An Angel of the Beatitudes

An Angel of the Beatitudes

Finding Faith After the Loss of a Child

Emily Ketring

Copyright © 2017 Emily Ketring
All rights reserved.
Scripture quotations are from the New Revised Standard Version Bible: Catholic Edition, copyright © 1989, 1993 the Division of Christian Education of the National Council of the Churches of Christ in the United States of America. Used by permission. All rights reserved.

Nihil Obstat
Hector R.G. Perez Robles, S.T.D.
Censor Librorum
Imprimatur:
Gregory L. Parkes, D.D., J.C.L.
Bishop of Pensacola-Tallahassee

ISBN: 1542627419
ISBN 13: 9781542627412

For my family, especially my three children and their father.

Contents

Acknowledgments · ix
Introduction · xi

A Mother's Heart; a Grieving Heart · 1
Our Angel · 6
My Darkest Night in All Its Terror · 14
Carmina's Poem · 19
I Am Israel, Struggling with God · 20
Grief · 24
Mother of Sorrow · 26
The Way of the Cross—Via Delarosa · 31
Joy and Pain are One · 37
Sister Death · 41
Faith, when all feels Hopeless · 45
Abandonment Draws Us Closer to Christ · · · · · · · · · · · · · · · · · · · 49
My God is a God of the Living · 54
Pilgrimage to Calvary · 57
Beyond the Language of the Living · 61
Anamnesis · 63
Heaven at the Center · 65
The Gift, Communion · 70
The Problem of Transformation · 72
"Why not me?" · 74

Be Not Afraid ·78
The Fallacy of Control · 80
Where is Heaven? ·83
A Child of the Beatitudes ·88

Acknowledgments

I AM INDEBTED to a host of authors and theologians who have unknowingly influenced my work and assisted me in my journey toward synthesizing my understanding of God's love at work in a world of suffering.

Thank you to Father Hector Perez Robles S.T.D., the Censor Librorum, who offered invaluable insight and resources toward the completed manuscript. Thank you to Bishop Gregory Parks, D.D., J.C.L. for the precious imprimatur of my beloved Church.

Special thanks to my sister, Naomi Sharp who offered me guidance and encouragement as she always does.

I want to express my most sincere gratitude to Angel's lifelong friend, Anna Kallschmidt for editing An Angel of the Beatitudes and working laboriously for six months checking and siting every source to ensure accuracy. Anna, I know Wife is pleased.

Introduction

My youngest child, my baby, Angel Olivia Ketring, entered eternity at the age of fifteen. A car accident claimed her beautiful life. She went with a friend to pick up another friend less than two miles away from our house and never made it back home. She did not even have her shoes on because she was coming right back…this life-shattering event, my great loss, has forever changed me and sent me on a challenging and painful spiritual journey. My faith was challenged, and I struggled with the very foundation of all my beliefs. I dared to ask if God is good, just, and trustworthy. My Great Loss served as an impetus to question God's nature, plan, and goodness; however, the questions were already in my heart. Like most of us, I had doubts that I dared not allow to surface until I was shaken to my knees. From this perspective, I no longer allowed God to remain unknown and with assumed goodness.

Every person must experience suffering to some degree. We all must share in the suffering of Christ. Suffering with Christ requires that one understand that God is good and working all things toward good. Sharing in Christ's suffering means that your suffering has value. The following pages delve into the mystery of suffering and how it is edifying and how it builds the Kingdom of God. The Paschal Mystery (Passion, death, and Resurrection of Jesus Christ) makes suffering an instrument of grace—not because suffering is good but because suffering is so terrible. God is always with us, loving us, and He uses everything toward good.

Finding comfort in suffering is of paramount importance, but to me the most important comfort in my Great Loss is understanding that Angel is still connected to me. Angel is still Angel—living a beautiful life that is more closely connected to me than ever before. Angel, and all those with Christ, are with us in a more intimate way because they are no longer limited by time and space. To find peace in suffering one must look beyond the finite and into the infinite and see the Divine Pattern of grace at work in all things, especially in suffering.

Sometimes God calls someone to be an instrument of his light; someone who shines in the darkness of this world and displays God's love—and Angel is one of those people. Angel imperfectly displayed God's love in a manner that is imitable, and her life is a wonderful example of living the Beatitudes in the twenty-first century. *An Angel of the Beatitudes* introduces a beautiful child, whose earthly life tragically ends, but her everlasting life shines through and displays God's glory. *An Angel of the Beatitudes* displays how suffering expands your very being, and the expansion enlarges your ability for love and joy and brings to life the most paradoxical beatitude: "blessed are those who mourn." (New Revised Standard Version Bible: Catholic Edition).[1]

---

1 Matt. 5:4 (New Revised Standard Version Bible: Catholic Edition).

A Mother's Heart; a Grieving Heart

We must love while we suffer, and we must suffer if we love.

—St. John Vianney[2]

---

2 Gretchen, Filz. "What St. John Vianney Taught About the Value of Suffering." Last modified February 26, 2017. https://www.catholiccompany.com/getfed/st-john-vianney-catechism-suffering/

THE FOLLOWING PAGES are reflections of my intimate grief journey. Actually, the following pages are what is in my heart translated into words. This journey is simultaneously my darkest hour and my greatest faith. It seems to me that my thoughts continue to culminate around two themes: trusting in God's goodness and the communion of saints. In my reflections you will see me vacillate from consolation to desolation and back to consolation. This is the nature of my grief and seems to be the nature of my faith. The following pages must be understood in the context of pain, grief, and a growing understanding of God. My faith journey is an extremely painful love story. Through this journey, I fell in love with God in the most intimate and sincere way. In the beginning, it is apparent I'm angry. I felt abandoned, and I wonder if God is a loving God. Actually, I feared that He was not the God of love. My deep-rooted fear came to the surface because I was afraid that Angel was not in the arms of love. I needed to face all my fears, and I address each of them in these pages.

Originally, I did not intend to share my writings. Writing my thoughts helped me process my grief and the theological issues that I was addressing. I have decided to share my reflections because I hope they may benefit another person who may be seeking Truth in earnest. I have strongly relied on the works of others in my spiritual growth, so I hope I am able to aid another person's journey.

It is imperative to understand that this work is progressive. It is an unfolding that does vacillate from consolation to desolation, and eventually it culminates in a sincere and heartfelt love. I had to go through all my feelings and questions; I had to struggle with my understanding of God. I began to question the nature of His goodness. These burning questions came from deep within my heart, and I know God was calling me *through my doubts*. God did not want me to repress my feelings and questions because any authentic relationship must be honest. Often honesty is painful.

I read many documents on suffering prior to my Great Loss, but suffering seemed more like a theological formula I was unable to solve. It seems that I had to experience my way toward understanding, and my understanding is more of acceptance than knowledge. Right after my Great Loss, my grief impeded me from finding meaning in suffering. I was so angry and hurt, and I wanted refuge from the pain. I didn't want to see any part of it as good. I simply needed and wanted a reprieve from suffering, so the redemptive power of suffering was undesirable. In time, I started to embrace my suffering as my constant companion, and I began to embrace its power for the Kingdom of God.

Due to my lack of understanding of the redemptive power of suffering, I was not comfortable with the Passion and death of Jesus Christ. This was a tremendous problem because it skewed my perception of God and I feared Him instead of loving Him. I could only see the terror of Calvary. I did not understand Christ's suffering, and I was unable to see it as beautiful—except that I knew it was Christ's selfless and total gift of Himself. Now I understand that my beautiful Lord used Himself to defeat death. Death is the ultimate division, the separation of the body and soul. God's will is to transform every division so "God may be all in all."[3] God used death and suffering, the consequences of sin, and transformed them into a channel of grace. Now death and suffering give us access to heaven where all divisions are healed and "all are all."[4] God used the worst to give us the best, and he is always working toward good. The way of the Cross is so difficult to see as an instrument of grace in our own lives. For that matter, it is difficult to see it as a grace at all. It is powerful, and it is not simply an instrument of grace for ourselves but an instrument of grace for many. Suffering builds up the Body of Christ through the communion of saints. The communion of saints is not individualistic, but communal. By virtue of solidarity, our suffering—like Christ's suffering—can help us and others. I offer my suffering for my children, my family, and my friends. I often offer my suffering for the unloved and for anyone who has been in such a state of poverty. I know that so much has been built up for the kingdom of heaven because I have infused my suffering to Mary's suffering at Calvary; therefore, my suffering is infused to Jesus's Passion.

---

[3] 1 Cor. 15:28.
[4] 1 Cor. 15:28.

In my reflections, it is obvious that I have a deep love and maternal pride for Angel; this is also true for my other children, John and Carmina. My husband Ward and I have always commented on how our children have seemed to inherit the best of each of us. So, admittedly, all these reflections are written through the lens of love, and I wouldn't have it any other way.

This is a letter I wrote to Angel, and I continue to talk and write to Angel. I continue my relationship with her, and I continue to express my deep love for her.

My Sweet Angel,

Everything in this world tells me that we are no longer connected and that you are gone from this world. My innermost being desires to talk with you, and I frequently speak with you, even though I'm never answered. Yet, day after day, I continue to foster a very real relationship, a relationship that transcends my natural senses. I know that the moment you were created, you became an immortal being who is not limited to matter. You were created for love, and you continue to live in Love. You entered the Divine relationship, and I am more connected to God through you. I long to be with you once again and touch and feel my beautiful baby. God gave us a body so we can use our senses, and we know that we will have a body in eternity; so, I will be able to touch you again. Jesus rose in the body, and he touched and he breathed and he ate and showed that he is not alive as a spirit only, but as a body. He gave the body dignity, immense dignity. I will feel you once again, and "all will be all."[5] We will be in full union without any separation. Love always seeks greater union because this is our eternal destiny: union.

The Spirit revealed to me that you are a Child of the Beatitudes. At first I really did not comprehend the meaning of the Beatitudes. I knew that they are a central part of Christ's teaching and that it is the Christian ideal to live the Beatitudes; however, I really did not have a concept of what that meant. To live the Beatitudes is to live the

---

5 1 Cor. 15:28.

Kingdom of God on earth. Now I understand the kingdom can only be described in paradoxical language.

As a child of the Beatitudes, you lived God's Kingdom with love and joy. You did not seek to be higher than anyone; you understood that no one was higher than you. You were not greedy; you just enjoyed life. You lamented other people's pain. You wanted a just world and participated in ensuring justice. Your mercy was severe. You were modest and pure. You always sought peace and understood its value. You would give yourself for another, even if your actions were not deserved. Indeed, you would suffer persecution for injustice as well as justice. You have uncompromising faith and an almost supernatural love. You embodied love that emanated joy—a Child of the Beatitudes. Now, you are a Child of the Beatitudes eternally, blessed and happy.

With all my love,

Mom

Our Angel

Sweetness and Humility

For me, this is all so very personal and I want to share my spiritual struggle, but I cannot do that without introducing Angel. I want everyone to get to know this wonderful child. My story is about her, and she is so much more than what happened to her. On the day of her funeral, I sent a quote to the local paper because I knew they were going to write about the accident, and I wanted the article to be about Angel instead of the accident. "Please convey just how extraordinary this child was. She was so very compassionate, and she was the most loving person. Her death is a true loss, not just for our family but for the entire world." Through my grief, I've realized two things: that Angel is still a gift to the entire world, and that she still exists—she *is* not she was. I refer to past events in Angel's life in the past tense, as that is proper for everyone and as Angel is alive in Christ; therefore, I refer to Angel as a person in the present tense.

Angel is a very loving person, and she is such a product of being the baby of our family. Angel did not have to be the strong one because Carmina and John were always strong for her. She is who she is mainly because of her siblings. Likewise, the good in Carmina and John is reflected in Angel and in each other. I am so very blessed to have three wonderful children—I mean, really blessed. I cannot change what happened, but I do know that the most important part of my children is the substance of who they are. As a mother, I have been greatly blessed with three children who are full of love and goodness—not that they are perfect, because I do not want the impossible, but the sum of who they are is beautiful. Angel's beautiful life continues.

Angel wrote this about her name:

> I was named by my sibling, my brother. Named after a God-sent messenger. The title gives me an edge, suits my personality, simply as well as my characteristics. The name I possess is "Angel." Every single T-shirt when I was a younger youth had my name on it. I wore it proudly. Doubts have filled others' minds. The name read off the roll call, "That can't possibly be her name." The name has five letters creating a word from the Bible: Angel.

Angel overcame extraordinary odds just to enter this world. My pregnancy was fraught with multiple complications, and I even had to have surgery while I was only seventeen weeks pregnant with her. I was on total bed rest, and I had a tumor that caused her premature birth. Angel entered this world with tubes and machines, and she left this life in the same manner. The years between these two events were full of love and joy. As mentioned, Angel is the baby of the family, and we cherish her as such; she is our gift. Angel's life was privileged because she was totally immersed in love.

It seems that God granted Angel a mature capacity of insight, compassion, and love. All mothers are proud of their children, but I knew Angel was extraordinary from a very young age. By the time she was three years old, she comprehended suffering and lamented it. She constantly performed acts of charity and gave herself as a gift. I look back now, and I'm amazed at all the acts of charity she performed in her short life. Angel's life was condensed to fifteen years, and it seems that God granted her the very mature gift of charity that usually takes years to develop.

A wonderful story about Angel that epitomizes her love was a conversation she had with her friend Nathan. (They were both about eight years old.) Nathan and Angel were talking about what they would do if a robber broke into their house. Nathan said he would kill the robber, and Angel said that Nathan should not kill him. Nathan argued stating that if he did not kill the robber, the robber would kill him. Angel said that it would be better "if he killed me because if he kills me, his soul is not ready to die." Young children do not think like this without the help of the Holy Spirit.

In some ways it feels particularly heinous that a child this wonderful, a child with so much to offer, was taken from this life. Words will never be capable of expressing the copious joy that she radiated here on earth. This feeling is derived from pride, and I know that. I also know that God is particularly fond of Angel, as he is of all his children.

This reminds me of something Angel said years ago when she was around seven years old. It was President's Day, and she said she did not want to celebrate. I asked her why and she said it was because presidents are people just like everyone else. She said, "Why don't we have a Poor

People Day?" She argued that they should not be honored just because they were important. She knows that all people deserve honor.

Angel and I co-chaired the Taylor County March of Dimes campaign in 2008. Angel was always willing to help others, and she raised money for many charities. My mother always said that Angel is the ambassador to the poor. Angel made a speech to encourage donations to the March of Dimes. She stated how she was thankful that people helped her as a premature baby. The very last thing Angel said to the crowd of grown-ups was "you can keep some dimes for yourself, or you can save a life." That is exactly how she sees justice. Another time, when she was in fifth grade, she encouraged her class to raise money for the refugees in Darfur. The local television station interviewed her, and she said, "People are dying over there, and I think we need to do something about it." She inspires people!

Emily and Angel Ketring during the March of Dimes Campaign

Angel's life exemplified love; however, she is not outwardly pious and certainly not judgmental. Angel has a great sense of humor, and her weakness was tasteless jokes. Angel knew how to live life to its fullest with great joy, and she is a wonderful example of how to live the Beatitudes today. Angel's way of living the Beatitudes did not separate her from people but, instead, more closely connected her. Angel, in imitation of Christ, always tries to include the excluded. I think sometimes we have images of holy people depicting a life of subdued holiness. Angel's holiness makes her happy, fun, and full of joy. Angel lived the gospel; she didn't preach it. Angel is not perfect, but her discipleship is just part of who she is. She is not intimidating. I think that is what is so appealing about her. She is genuine; she accepts the imperfections of others, and this acceptance attracts people to her.

Angel is best introduced through her own words. I have included a few things that she wrote that I think offers a glimpse of her personality. I want to share this beautiful child and allows others to get to know her because to know her is to love her.

Angel's Confirmation Journal
By Angel Ketring

(One thing) I want to learn in my confirmation year is learning to deal with bad influences. Also, when Catholicism is a small parish in Perry, to learn to stay away from the other sixty-six churches. It's important to keep in mind God's love for us under peer pressure. To learn the deep meaning of heaven/God and to learn my patron saint.

On the first day of confirmation class, the priest asked the class, "What does God look like to you?" Angel raised her hand, and Father called on her. Angel said, "I see God as a giant face with a bunch of tiny faces that make his face." I was dumbfounded at her response because I knew that she has a magnificent understanding of the communion of saints. Her wisdom far exceeded her years.

Angel's Eighth-Grade Paper
By Angel Ketring

I'm Angel Olivia Ketring, also known as AOK. I was born in Tallahassee Memorial Hospital. My due date was July 16 (the same day as my cousin). I was born early on May 23, 1997. I was born early because my mom had a tumor on her ovary. At that time my grandpa was supposed to die anytime and my cousin was struggling from being premature and so was I. None of us died—my grandpa, my cousin, and I. Ever since my life has been great.

I have played a variety of instruments: the glockenspiel, violin, and piano. I have not succeeded with moving forward with any of these instruments. I have done many sports and teams: Academic Team, baton, gymnastics, and cheerleading. I have chosen to stay with Academic Team and baton.

I have one brother and one sister. I own a double-seater bike that my sister and I ride through town occasionally.

I like to discuss theology, history, and also anything interesting that I just learned about.

AN ENTHUSIASTIC, LOVING HYPOCRITE

Angel wrote two poems about herself for English class. One is about being an enthusiastic young female, and the other described herself as a loving hypocrite. Angel and Carmina always said that everyone has at least a little hypocrisy. I love the way she embraced the imperfection of hypocrisy.

I am a Loving Hypocrite
Angel Ketring

I am a loving hypocrite.
I visualize a future helping those in need.
I hear my patient's broken voices.
I observe their hectic position.
I anticipate to become the best occupational therapist.
I am a loving hypocrite.
I seem like an ambitious runner.
I feel the striking impact on my feet from the dirt road.
I touch the finish line with my stomach as it snaps in my presence.
I disapprove of those who quit.
I weep when I do not break my personal record.
I am a loving hypocrite.
I understand that life comes with unpleasant difficulties.
I represent being pro-life.
I demonstrate happiness through life's dips.
I challenge to be well rounded.
I hope to better my generation.
I am a loving hypocrite.

I am a Driven Enthusiastic Young Female
Angel Ketring

I am a driven enthusiastic young female…
I wonder about the ecstatic road ahead of me.
I hear dedication pushing myself forth.
I see my life in ten years with many mistakes as well as accomplishments.
I want to make a best friend.
I am a driven enthusiastic young female.
I pretend I know what I'm doing.
I feel anxiety beating down like the blistering sun.
I touch ambition to live life to its fullest.
I worry about losing a relationship with my siblings.
I cry when I have fatigue.
I am a driven enthusiastic young female.
I understand that life may be rough.
I say that I am a Catholic.
I dream about how life will turn out.
I try to present satisfaction to others.
I am a driven enthusiastic young female.

My Darkest Night in All Its Terror

The more we suffer, the more we are favored by God.[6]

—St. Jane Frances de Chantal

Ward woke me up in a panic telling me that Angel had been in an accident. I jumped up and ran to the car, without any shoes and wearing only lightweight pajamas. Angel went with her friend Jimmy to pick up their friend, Cody, who lived just a few miles away. Someone had called us and informed Ward that she was in an accident. Ward, Carmina, and I rushed to the scene. I jumped out of the car and ran into the chaos of a major accident. Somehow I immediately found the ambulance that carried Angel, and a police officer named Lynn Gray grabbed me and prevented me from going to her. I realized that the accident was severe, and I fell on my knees to pray on the spot. My husband and daughter, Carmina, approached the ambulance, and Ward demanded that they transport her to the hospital because he was afraid that we were losing valuable time.

---

6 Francis De Sales, Wendy M. Wright, and Joseph F. Power, "Letters of Spiritual Direction," in *Francis de Sales, Jane de Chantal: Letters of Spiritual Direction*, ed. Theresa M. Sparacio. (New Jersey: Paulist Press, 1998), 207.

AN ANGEL OF THE BEATITUDES

Carmina and I rode to the hospital with Officer Gray and when we got there they were about to take her from the ambulance. Lynn asked me to pray and this distracted me while they moved her inside. Later Carmina told me that she witnessed them doing CPR on her in the ambulance. The hospital staff refused to allow us in the back. I was not ready to receive people, so the only person I felt compelled to call was Father Bernie to ask that he come to give her the anointing of the sick. I was afraid to deal with anyone else. My parents and my brother arrived very soon, and when my mother came in crying I just held up my hand and said, "No." I just could not fall apart.

Cody's mother, who was in the back seat of the car (he was also in the accident with Angel) suddenly opened the locked door that prevented me from being with Angel; she grabbed me and took me to the back and told me, "They are doing CPR on your baby and I had to come get you." I asked her, "Where is she?" and she led me to her. I remember the room was full of people and I realized that they needed to work on her. The room had glass doors and glass around the door, so I could see everything that was happening. I remember I wanted to stay out of their way, so I stayed in the hallway because I did not want to impede their efforts to save her life. I remember Officer Gray grabbing me, and I told him that I was alright; I just need to be here. I dropped to my knees and prayed, as I watched them perform CPR for maybe fifteen minutes. I remember someone straddled her while doing chest compressions. I remember being on the floor and realizing that I was dying too. I knew that I was as low as I'd ever been. I actually remember knowing I was barefoot and in thin pajamas, and I wanted to feel naked and exposed. This may be a hard concept to grasp, but all pride seemed absurd, and I wanted no part of it. A longtime family friend was a nurse on duty and she wrapped a blanket around me. It was such a beautiful act of kindness and it was done without an exchange of words.

Suddenly, everyone was clapping as they had got her heartbeat back. I remained nervous, but I thought she was going to make it. Eventually, Ward, my mom, and my sister-in-law came to the back with me. I didn't tell them what had happened; I thought it was too horrible to dare utter. Father came and anointed her. Finally, they allowed us to approach her and her head had so many tubes, so I kissed her feet. When I touched her, she was cold, but I still hoped. When doctors approached me my only question was, "Is there hope?" One doctor said, "There is always hope." So I hoped and begged God to save her.

Ward, Carmina, and I left for Tallahassee, about fifty miles away, because they were going to transport her, and we wanted to be on the other side for her. My son, John, wanted to stay with her until she left so she was never without one of us. I remember just holding Carmina and telling her that I was sorry that she had to go through this. We prayed the entire drive and I actually remember thinking during the Our Father that I was on dangerous territory. When I stated, "thy will be done," I knew that His will may be my greatest fear realized. I said the prayer anyway, and I even had guilt because I wondered if I should have protested His will. I went with my instinct to surrender. Later, I wondered if that was a mistake. The Holy Spirit led me and the Virgin was beside me in my darkest hour.

When we arrived in Tallahassee we found out that they could not transport her yet. No one was clear about what was happening. A wonderful chaplain was there with us and he asked if we wanted him to call a priest. He called a nearby priest named Father Tim. Providentially, we knew Father Tim for a long time even before he was ever a priest. Father Tim arrived and waited and prayed with us. A nurse came in to inform us that she was inflight, but she had stopped breathing and they were performing CPR. Inside, I realized that they were preparing us, but I hoped. Finally, a doctor came to tell us that she did not make it, and all the family started lamenting. I remember that I needed to get away from the crying, and I asked to see her. Father Tim and I went into the room where she was. I put my hands on her, and I thanked God for her, and I gave her back to God. I thanked God for her over and over again. I just continued to kiss her entire body and tell her I loved her. Father and I would also pray. I remember I told Father Tim that I was still going to be close to her in the Eucharist. At her death bedside, I knew the Eucharist was my connection to her. Ward, John, Carmina, my mother and my mother-in-law eventually came in to see her. I just kept kissing her all over. I remember thinking that it was a holy experience. I knew I was in liminal space, on holy ground. I stayed for a long time with her just kissing her, telling her that I loved her. Later, I told John and Carmina that I did not want them haunted by that image. Angel's life was covered in love, and I just wanted her death to also be covered by love. That night was my heartbreak that would never heal.

I went into the lobby, and I stated that I will not accept flowers. Angel always cared for others, so I wanted donations for the Divine Mercy Center (Angel often raised money for Divine Mercy, a food pantry run by our church). I wanted everything to remain humble that was in connection to Angel. I emphatically reminded everyone that Angel was a gift and I've held onto that truth.

Within hours of being home, I vividly remembered a thought that I received, and it was that Angel was a child of the Beatitudes. I'd never thought about it before, but when the thought came to me I realized that it was true. Angel, a child of the Beatitudes. The Beatitudes—supreme blessedness. The blessings listed by Jesus in the Sermon on the Mount (Matt. 5:3–11).

Just hours later, we went to the funeral home to make arrangements. My brother, my sister-in-law, my mother, my husband, my sister, and my son, John, met in the funeral home, and I refused to go through the entire process. All I wanted was a funeral mass; every other decision was unimportant to me. First, the funeral director tried to talk me out of having the funeral so soon. The funeral was about thirty hours after her death. It was supposed to rain, but I would not budge. I just wanted to get the funeral over with as soon as possible because I knew it was going to be so painful. So with heavy rain expected, the funeral was set. The funeral director said we needed to pick a casket, but I refused. I stated that I did not care what she was buried in, and I could tell that they did not know what to do with me. The only two things I chose were to have her thumbprint made into a necklace and the Saint Francis poem on the inside of her funeral card. Unknown to me at that time, my son, John, chose everything for his Angel, and my brother stayed with him to make the arrangements.

Father Crawford came to see me the night before the funeral, and I was very interested in planning the funeral mass. Ward was in there with us for a while, but he let me make the decisions on the mass, and he left us alone. I vividly remember Father telling me, "God loves you this much." I did not understand what he meant, but I held it in my heart. We discussed the psalms, but I do not remember what we decided. Father was discussing the Gospel reading, and he recommended the Pearl of Saint Matthew[7] because he knew I was going to need Christ to help me carry my burden. I needed Christ to be eye to eye with me. I was moved by this gospel. He also suggested the Gospel of the Beatitudes[8], and I knew that it had to be the Beatitudes and so it was.

Many of the kids at school decided to wear white in honor of Angel, so I decided I was to wear white as well. I wore Angel's Confirmation dress to her funeral. We sat there through the mass with her beside us in her casket. Over six hundred people were in attendance, and most people stood in the rain for two hours. Most of the rest of it is a blur, but I do remember on the way to the graveside that it was pouring rain, and the officers who blocked the roads were standing in attention in the pouring rain. I was so touched.

Hundreds of people stood in the rain to attend Angel's funeral

---

7 Matt. 13:45-46
8 Matt. 5:3-12

Carmina's Poem

Angel was born in May and died in September. The lily of the valley is May's flower, and the morning glory and the aster are September's. Lily of the valley stands for "sweetness and humility" and used to be sent as a message saying, "You've made my life complete." The aster used to be sent to say, "Take care of yourself for me."

> I still feel you with me
> Even though your heart doesn't beat.
> Here for so little time
> You've made my life complete.
> You came into my life with
> Sweetness and humility.
> One day we will unite
> My Lily of the Valley.
>
> I see the Morning has lost the glory
> Night has come and you have died.
> Such a beauty with a life so short
> The sun has set from the sunrise.
> The Aster comes to be, and says
> "Take care of yourself for me."

I Am Israel, Struggling with God

Suffering for God is better than working miracles[9]

—St. John of the Cross

I see Jesus as my brother and friend; my savior. I understand that He gave the human race His total gift of self on the Cross. Love as self-gift is only understood through mature love. It used to bother me that Jesus had to suffer for our salvation because I didn't understand that love always requires sacrifice. Now, I certainly get that concept. What I still do not understand is why God would require His son to die for us? I believe that it is imperative to be honest about the questions and doubts in your heart, so you can grow in faith and love of God.

The very famous verse, John 3:16, explains a love that I do not understand: "For God loved the world so much that He gave His one and only Son, so that everyone who believes in Him will not perish but have eternal life."[10] God gave His Son for love, but this bothers me because that does not sound

---

[9] Saint John of the Cross, *The Collected Works of St. John of the Cross*, trans. Kieran Kayanaugh and Otilio Rodriguez (Washington D.C.: Institute of Carmelite Studies, 1991), 64.

[10] John 3:16.

like a paternal act of love. I know that the Trinity is one and that Jesus came to reveal the true nature of God, but I am still bewildered by the Father willingly sacrificing His Son, even if it is for the good of others. In fact, in moral theology, the end never justifies the means. Even when I look at nature, many animals are protective of their young; therefore, natural law seems to reiterate the protective nature of a parent. Because God loves us so much that He did not spare His only Son is a very difficult concept for me.

I do realize that I am asking these questions with my limited human mind that is incapable of fully understanding God. The ways of God are not like the ways of man, but He revealed this sacrifice to us for a reason. I also understand that a great deal of religious truth is conveyed in metaphor and paradox that reveals a spiritual truth. God revealed the Crucifixion as the central act in salvation history. The centrality of it makes me think that I am supposed to comprehend this as an act of love, yet I never have. I see the Holy Spirit as my advocate, my comforter, and Jesus as my loving savior who gave the total gift of Himself. Honestly, I've always been afraid of God, the Father.

I fear Him because I thought He willed the horrific death of His own Son. It seems that no one is safe, not even His Son. As a parent this is incomprehensible. I would do *anything* to have been able to prevent Angel's death. Yet, Jesus prayed for this cup to pass Him but acquiesced to the Father's will. It seems like my love for Angel is the kind of love that is good. The death of a child created a much greater need for me to understand this event in light of charity (love) because it seemed so wrong. I was so afraid that Angel was not safe because even Jesus was not safe from God. I understand that I am a creature and He is God, but I also know that He has revealed Himself so we are able to have a relationship with Him. I realized that I needed more understanding.

Jesus teaches us that He displayed the love of the Father. He said, "Whoever has seen me has seen the Father."[11] Jesus displays perfect love, and He and the Father are one. God, the Father, and the Son's relationship differs from my relationship with Angel. Angel and I are not one. So this, I believe, is why I have so much trouble comprehending the Crucifixion. I am seeking

---

11 John 14:9.

understanding through the lens of love, and I believe that it is imperative to be honest about the questions and doubts in your heart, so you can grow in Faith and Love of God.

I believe that death is a mercy and it inaugurates our everlasting life; therefore, death is not bad because we really do not believe in it. Death entered the world through Satan and man, but death does not have the last word; life does. Many religious truths are conveyed in paradox, so I attempt to look at paradox to understand. When I hear people state John 3:16 as a verse of love, I continue to know my experience contradicts this, but I look to other paradoxes for understanding. I know that the Beatitudes are paradoxical, but nothing seems contrary to charity. The Crucifixion is the paradox that I have trouble comprehending as an act of love. I suppose that I separate God and Jesus too much because it is such a mystery that cannot be fully grasped. I understand the self-gift of Jesus; however, I do not understand why God asked it of His Son. Again, the problem may be in my perception of God as Father in relation to the Son.

Now, more than ever, it is important for me to understand this in the light of charity. I want to know that my sweet Angel is with a loving Father. I am struggling with these questions because I want a greater understanding. I hope my search for understanding deepens my relationship with God. I think of Jacob and the very name "Israel" (struggle with God).[12] I used to think that it was wrong to question God's goodness; however, I am seeking God in earnest. Pope Benedict's book *Introduction of Christianity* addresses the questioning of faith and assures us that questioning is the way to greater faith. I do not think my faith can be shaken; I believe. What I am trying to understand is the nature of God, the Father, as a loving Father. I remain faithful to God in spite of these questions because I believe He is good. The hope inside me knows He must be good.

Petition prayer is very difficult for me now, and I think this is the case for three reasons: first, I am unsure of God's goodness; second, it seems that God's plan is already set, and it does not seem that our prayer changes that plan. It's almost as if we think we have control of God. I realize that He is

---

12 Gen. 32:28.

taking care of Angel, and that is the true nature of my prayer, but it still makes me feel as if my prayers do not matter. The third part of my struggle is that some people have their prayers answered, and their children survive. Why not Angel?

I know that the answer to this question is in God's mystery. Again, if I feel that God is totally good, perhaps I can trust Him more. I've always had difficulty with petition prayer because I have always thought that God is going to do what is best and is most loving even without any prayer whatsoever. God is good all the time and he does not need to be convinced of acting in an altruistic manner. God is immutable, and prayer does not change God, but prayer changes man; therefore, prayer changes history. It is an act of love to pray for others, so it builds up charity. For the sake of charity, all petition prayer is good.

God is immutable love, but He wants a relationship with us. He wants us to talk to Him, to share with Him, to open our hearts to Him. Part of that relationship is petition prayer; however, we do not change God. God changes us. For example, praying for the health and well-being of another person is never in vain. God's immutable love is not changed by the amount or sincerity of our petition. We do not control God, and God chooses not to control us. Petition prayer is part of a loving relationship that God always molds toward good, in love.

Grief

> (Grief is) lonely, isolating: many times, it feels
> like it's just me and the universe and God.
>
> —Karen Warren[13]

GRIEF IS NOT static and it continues because losses continue to occur. September 16, 2012, the day of my Great Loss, set off a chain reaction of loss that continues to take from my family. Every event or holiday is grief anew because it is lost.

Every Christmas, we continue to celebrate as we always have, but our sweet Angel is missing in her bodily presence. We continue to enjoy the company of family, but with a heavy heart because nothing feels complete anymore. We miss her so much, and as the years pass we miss her more and more. Angel still belongs to our family, so her missing presence continues to create new forms of grief.

No one would dare approach the Virgin on Holy Saturday and expect anything but sorrow. People are so uncomfortable with sorrow and people

---

13 Michelle A. Vu. "Kay Warren on Son's Suicide: 'This Is Not How It Should Be,' But Grateful That Matthew's 'Broken Mind' Is Now Healed in Heaven." Accessed November 21, 2016. http://www.christianpost.com/news/kay-warren-on-sons-suicide-this-is-not-how-it-should-be-but-grateful-that-matthews-broken-mind-is-now-healed-in-heaven-109441/.

want you to move through it as if it is something to be overcome. The sorrow becomes an intrinsic part of you and all you can do is embrace it. You do experience joy that permeates the sadness, but the sorrow returns. I think the joy is sweeter than ever before and valued as a precious gift. It's just a different life that I believe Christ is using for His greater glory. Many people want you to "be strong" and I really do not know what that means. I think people are so uncomfortable with grief, so they want you to get through it quickly. Other people tire from your grief and you tire from it too, but that doesn't change that it is there.

People will often say, "I just don't know how you do it." Sometimes they even say that they would be unable to handle losing a child. I want to scream, "I don't 'do it'! It was done to me!" One thing I do know is that I am not in control. Tragedy is something that happens to you, and you are simply left with what is.

Often people tell me that I'm handling everything so well, and their words actually make me angry. I realize they do not mean to be hurtful, but to me their statements presuppose a standard of good grieving. Grief just is. I realize sometimes people grieve in ways that can become self-destructive, but even that type of grief may be necessary for that person. I do not show my grief to others, so they have no idea of how I am really doing. I wish people would not assume that they know what I'm feeling.

Grief is very sensitive. I know people are trying to say things that are helpful, but often they inadvertently hurt you. When a person is grieving, just love him or her. Do not try to fix it or relate to it; just be present for the person. Say you are sorry—because you are—and then just let them grieve. Love them in their grief.

Deep grief is so much stronger than I am, and I cannot use my own willpower to overcome it. It is a burden that is too heavy, so any display of strength is derived from Christ in me, not from me. All I can do is surrender to the pain and sorrow and ask Christ to carry me to Easter. I hope that Christ will restore all that I have lost, and this is how any joy is possible after tragedy. Joy after tragedy is always derived from hope.

The big wave at the ocean that pulls you under... again + again...

Mother of Sorrow

Mary, mother of love and human pain

—John Paul II[14]

---

14 Pope John Paul II, "Mary is Model of Care for the Sick," *L'Osservatore Romano*, November 8, 1995, accessed November 22, 2016, https://www.ewtn.com/library/PAPALDOC/JP951101.HTM

AN ANGEL OF THE BEATITUDES

September 14 is my birthday, the feast of the triumph of the Cross. September 16 is Angel's feast day, but September 15 is in between, and it is the feast of Our Lady of Sorrow. It is hard to find peace and joy with an irreparable broken heart. I have moments of joy, but the pain is still there. Pain is the only constant; every other emotion vacillates. I am close to the Mother of Sorrow.

I feel in solidarity with the Virgin Mother. She, like me, had to watch her beloved child die. She had no choice in the matter. I was present as they did CPR on my baby. All I could do was pray, and that is what I did. I was present, like the Virgin. Like her, I was helpless. I know that Mary leads us closer to Jesus, but the Father is still obscured to me. Perhaps it is because I feel that He did not answer my prayers. I do realize that Angel's death might be a mercy, and it helps me when I think of that. I think I want reassurance about God's love because I want to trust the love that now holds her. I want to be assured that God is love.

I am Rachel: "A voice is heard in Ramah, mourning and great weeping, Rachel weeping for her children and refusing to be comforted, because they are no more."[15] I am Rachel, but Rachel mourned before the Resurrection. My dear Angel is still with us; she is alive in Christ who defeated death. Rachel did not have hope because Christ had not yet come. Mothers instinctively protect their children, and we hope for our children's future. Children are our immortality and we desire a posterity that continues long after we are gone. When your child is taken from this life, all hope of a future on earth is crushed, and all that is left is the past. This heartbreaking reality is a disappointment of paramount significance. It may easily lead to despair and leave you in sadness that is devoid of Christian joy. The word "disappointment" fails to connote the emotion associated with this loss. This disappointment feels as if it is despair, the antithesis of hope.

I now clearly realize that the destiny of all our children is a bodily death. My Angel preceded me in her walk into eternity, but that is just a matter of timing. All parents want to precede their children's death because a child's death is so very painful. No parent really wants to think about the mortality

---

15 Jer. 31:15.

of his or her children, but the only guarantee our children have in this life is an imminent bodily death. People are constantly telling me how horrific Angel's death must be, and it is…but not because she left this world. It's horrific because she left this world before me. We almost view our children as our immortality, but our immortality is from God.

My point is this: I realize that wanting to die before my children is somewhat selfish, and it contradicts the selflessness that being a mother requires. Our children must leave this earth, and God will take them in His time. Angel's time preceded mine, but my hope is that it is what is best for her eternal life. My pain is a deep emotion that stems from an altruistic love—and that is not wrong, and it will remain with me. I have realized that losing Angel is terrible because of me, not her. It is just a matter of timing; it is not as if she could have permanently avoided death. Indeed, none of us will.

Perhaps losing a child requires more self-giving love. It requires you to realize that death is not about you; it's about the other person. Angel's destiny is no different than anyone else's. What happened to her will happen to us all, even our children. It helps me to realize that her bodily death was an unavoidable event; the only real difference of an early death is that I must suffer her loss on this earth. That puts me at the center, and I will never find peace when I put myself in that position. Now, I'm in the challenging position of accepting Angel's walk into eternity, as a mother. This is an enormous task! A task that will require a selfless love. It may require the quintessential motherly love.

As a mother, the very theology of our bodies reveals that love must suffer. The birthing process is painful for the mother and for the child. Children are our love incarnate, and love must come to life through suffering.

The blood of our loved ones is always precious. The blood of your baby is far beyond precious. Like the very name of God, its value is ineffable. For this reason, I perceive Mary's suffering at Calvary as even greater than Christ's suffering because her heart was pierced with the deepest and most painful sword. She was spiritually crucified, and watching her dear child suffer was far worse than suffering the pain herself. I realize that Christ's suffering under the full weight of our sins was suffering beyond even Mary's, but I know she would have taken it upon herself if she could. This humble mother was always present—from Christ's birth to His death, to His Resurrection. I try to find peace in her. I am not like Mary in virtue, but I am like her in suffering the loss of a beloved child. She is my companion.

To understand suffering, it must be recognized as a mystery in which we are called to participate. "Every man has his own share in the Redemption. Each one is also called to share in that suffering through which the Redemption was accomplished. He is called to share in that suffering through which all human suffering has also been redeemed. In bringing about the Redemption through suffering, Christ has also raised human suffering to the level of the Redemption. Thus each man, in his suffering, can also become a sharer in the redemptive suffering of Christ."[16]

I offer my suffering to God and I hope it has value. I hope that the deep pain will expand my ability to be united with God and Angel. Perhaps eternity will be greater because of this life sentence of pain. It seems the closer you are to God, the greater your suffering. Look at the Bible and Jesus's Blessed Mother. I think about Mary so much, and I know she was the perfect disciple, but how did she feel? Did she feel that God chose her for suffering and pain? Did she feel abandoned? When we say that she is blessed among all women, I wonder if she felt the same. She was still human with limited understanding, and I think she must have felt that God had called her to suffer. He broke her, and we do not know how she felt.

Her last recorded words were "Do whatever he tells you."[17] Indeed, this statement is beautiful and shows us her perfect discipleship, but it does not tell us about her feelings. All we know is that in the end, she always did what was right. That doesn't mean she understood the journey. It doesn't mean she

---

16 Pope John Paul II, "Salvifici Doloris." Last modified February 11, 1984. https://w2.vatican.va/content/john-paul-ii/en/apost_letters/1984/documents/hf_jp-ii_apl_11021984_salvifici-doloris.html

17 John 2:5.

didn't feel abandoned by God. I pray that my difficult journey is all for good because it feels so dark.

The Cross is simultaneously the greatest and the worst thing in history. Christ makes all things new. He transforms the worst to make it the best, and I know that is connected to suffering. "Offer suffering to God, and it can become 'an instrument of salvation, a path to holiness, that helps us reach heaven.'"[18]

---

18 Pope John Paul II, "Salvifici Doloris." Last modified February 11, 1984. https://w2.vatican.va/content/john-paul-ii/en/apost_letters/1984/documents/hf_jp-ii_apl_11021984_salvifici-doloris.html

The Way of the Cross—Via Delarosa

> If one becomes a sharer in the sufferings of Christ, this happens because Christ has opened his suffering to man, because He Himself in His redemptive suffering has become, in a certain sense, a sharer in all of human sufferings.
>
> —Pope John Paul II[19]

Jesus, in His great mercy, came to show us the way. Jesus lived His life for others and gave Himself as a complete gift. His way is love. Right before He died he said, "It is finished." What was finished? His earthly life was completed because He showed us the Way and gave Himself as a total gift. His gift is our redemption, but the Way is through the gift of selfless Love. Angel's life was not cut short, it was finished. Her life was a gift and she gave herself to others. She was embodied love, a total gift. The night she died Carmina said, "Angel is glad that it was she who died and not another." I knew that it is true —Wow

---

19 Pope John Paul II, "Salvifici Doloris." Last modified February 11, 1984. https://w2.vatican.va/content/john-paul-ii/en/apost_letters/1984/documents/hf_jp-ii_apl_11021984_salvifici-doloris.html

that Angel is happy that she was the one taken. Indeed, "It was finished."[20] The hospital requested that we consider donating all that was viable, so we did. It was a perfect metaphor for Angel and her total gift of self. Her body was even salvaged for the good of others. Her body was a gift in death and her body remains important and part of her.

> "Man cannot fully find himself except through a sincere gift of himself." It is easy to turn in on oneself when we experience suffering. At times it can consume our souls, focusing too much on our pain and suffering. This should not be the case. Suffering, when patiently endured and united with Christ's passion, gradually causes us to go out of ourselves, giving the very gift of our suffering for the sake of others. The cross is not a selfish gift but extreme selflessness in the act of love."[21]

The crucifixion has always been a problem for me because I could not comprehend why the violence against Jesus was necessary. In fact, I had such an individualistic view that I didn't understand how the human race is connected. To me, His suffering for my sake seemed absurd. I used to wonder if others felt the same. Once I realized the solidarity of the human race, I was able to comprehend that the crucifixion's effects can be transmitted through our solidarity, through our oneness. Adam's sin brought death and suffering to the entire human race and creation. Sin and death were not what God wanted for the world, but as God always does, He made something *good* out of something evil. When God created the world, "It was good."[22] The *Fall* introduced suffering and death. It required a savior and God gave us something greater than we had before the *Fall*; we are now sons and daughters of God. We are now

---

20 John 19:30.
21 Pope John Paul II, "Salvifici Doloris." Last modified February 11, 1984. https://w2.vatican.va/content/john-paul-ii/en/apost_letters/1984/documents/hf_jp-ii_apl_11021984_salvifici-doloris.html
22 Gen. 1:10.

able to share in the very life of the Blessed Trinity. Our savior is our brother; He is Emmanuel, God with us.

Through all these reflections, I still remained bothered about why violence against the son was necessary. I understood Jesus's total gift of self, but why suffering and death? Quite frankly, the entire crucifixion seemed extremely malicious. Again, when I'd hear people say that God loved us so much that He gave His only son for us and they seemed to think it was an act of love, I felt dumbfounded. It always sounded horrible to me, and I wondered why it seemed altruistic to others. It seemed absurd to me, but everyone seemed to think that it was a logical conclusion. At the same time, I'd ask for help understanding it and the answer was usually about atonement and that the price of sin had to be paid. I wondered, paid to whom or what and why? This does not sound like a loving God and how can we trust Him if He willed the horrific death of His beloved son? This is honestly how I felt and I was unable to reconcile this reality of our faith. This was my most agonizing thought because it undermined my belief that God is a loving Father.

Finally, with the help of Church teaching, I feel that I have pierced the veil of understanding that is consistent with a loving God. "From the greatest moral evil ever committed, the rejection and murder of God's only Son, caused by the sins of all men—God, by his grace that 'abounded all the more,' brought the greatest of goods: the glorification of Christ and our redemption"[23]. God did not "will the horrific death of His beloved Son." God's will is not death: it is Life. God sent Christ to Love and to offer Life. The consequences of sin are suffering and death; therefore, Christ came and offered us salvation through suffering and death. He used the consequence as the instrument of salvation thereby giving the effects of sin an edifying power. He used the worst to give us the best. Precisely because it is the worst, it produces the best.

Christ voluntarily came and innocently suffered. Christ's will is united, as it always is, to the will of the Father. The will of God is always Love and Life. God sent Christ so man may witness Love incarnate. Sometimes the

---

[23] IntraText Editorial Staff, eds., *Catechism of the Catholic Church*. (Citta del Vaticano: Libreria Editrice Vaticana, 1993), accessed November 11, 2016, http://www.vatican.va/archive/ENG0015/_INDEX.HTM#fonte.

language used to explain why Christ came makes it sound as if God needed a sacrifice so He sent His only beloved Son. This perspective is problematic! For me, this perspective made me untrusting and fearful of the Father. I feared my sweet Angel was with an unloving Father and it scared me. Now I know that God did not will "the greatest moral evil ever committed."[24] God is a loving Father. He sent Christ in Love; Christ showed us how to love and offered us salvation through suffering. Suffering is no longer just a consequence of sin, but a means of transmitting grace. Suffering is no longer just terrible because suffering may be united to the suffering passion of our Lord.

> "For God so loved the world that He gave His only Son, that whoever believes in Him should not perish but have eternal life.[23]" Christ goes toward His own suffering, aware of its saving power; He goes forward in obedience to the Father, but primarily He is united to the Father in this love with which He has loved the world and man in the world. And for this reason Saint Paul will write of Christ: "He loved me and gave Himself for me."[25]
>
> Christ suffers voluntarily and suffers innocently. With his suffering he accepts that question which—posed by people many times—has been expressed, in a certain sense, in a radical way by the Book of Job. Christ, however, not only carries with himself the same question (and this in an even more radical way, for he is not only a man like Job but the only-begotten Son of God), but he also carries the greatest possible answer to this question. One can say that this answer emerges from the very master of which the question is made up. Christ gives the answer to the question about suffering and the meaning of suffering not only by his teaching, that is by the good news, but most of all by his own suffering, which is integrated with this teaching of the

---

24 John 3:16
25 IntraText Editorial Staff, eds., *Catechism of the Catholic Church.* (Citta del Vaticano: Libreria Editrice Vaticana, 1993), accessed November 11, 2016, http://www.vatican.va/archive/ENG0015/_INDEX.HTM#fonte.

good news in an organic and indissoluble way. And this is the final, definitive word of this teaching: "the word of the Cross," as Saint Paul one day will say[26].

I also realized that God the Father could not be with us in the same manner as our brother Christ is able to be with us. Our brother gave us the grace to be assimilated into the very life of God. A Father is a different relationship than a brother; this task required a brother that is "like us in all things except sin."[27] He became sin and rendered its effects impotent. God's, the Father, Son and Holy Spirit, will is to defeat death and offer everlasting life. God beautifully uses sin's consequences as a medium for grace and redemption. The pain has purpose and power. In *Why Does God Permit Evil*, Bruno Webb explains:

> All suffering that takes place in us draws its supernatural value from the suffering He endured in His passion. On Calvary Christ used suffering as the instrument by which He won for us the grace of redemption. By doing this He sanctified human suffering for all time and has given suffering a quasi-sacramental value. That is to say, whenever He permits any suffering whatever, be it great or small, to come to any of us, that suffering comes to us as a channel of grace…By our sufferings He transmits grace to us[28]. -
> He has set His grasp upon suffering itself, the penalty of sin, universally and in all its forms, making of it an interment by means of which man can merit a higher bliss in Heaven than he ever could have done had there been no sin and suffering. Christ did not destroy this

---

26 Pope John Paul II, "Salvifici Doloris." Last modified February 11, 1984. https://w2.vatican.va/content/john-paul-ii/en/apost_letters/1984/documents/hf_jp-ii_apl_11021984_salvifici-doloris.html

27 Council of Chalcedon (451): DS 301; cf. Heb 4:15.
IntraText Editorial Staff, eds., *Catechism of the Catholic Church*.(Citta del Vaticano: Libreria Editrice Vaticana, 1993), accessed November 11, 2016, http://www.vatican.va/archive/ENG0015/_INDEX.HTM#fonte.

28 Dom Bruno Webb, *Why Does God Permit Evil?* (Manchester: Sophia Institute Press, 2004), 100.

terrible offspring of sin, but with infinitely greater power and wisdom, with greater generosity and love for us, has used it universally as a means of drawing from evil an immeasurably greater good for man[29].

The more our life conforms to Christ's own life on earth, the closer we are "oned" with Him, the more fully do we cooperate in His own redemptive work for the salvation of souls, and the richer will be our share in His glory in a life that has no end[30].

Although Christ is not present on earth in his physical body, he is present within each of us who are members of his mystical body, the Church. In and through us Christ suffers. Our suffering is truly a participation in the passion of Christ. "Christ achieved the Redemption completely and to the very limit; but at the same time He did not bring it to a close."[31]

---

29 Ibid, 128.
30 Ibid
31 Pope John Paul II, "Salvifici Doloris." Last modified February 11, 1984. https://w2.vatican.va/content/john-paul-ii/en/apost_letters/1984/documents/hf_jp-ii_apl_11021984_salvifici-doloris.html

Joy and Pain are One

[T]here the greater shall be our joy, the
more we have suffered here below.

—Pope St. Gregory[32]

Angel being silly and always full of joy

---

32 Pope Saint Gregory. "A Journey to the Catholic Church." Last modified March 24, 2016. http://chnetwork.org/story/a-journey-to-the-catholic-church/

I ONCE READ that the wells of pain and joy within us are not separate. With that in mind; the greater your pain, the greater is your ability to be joyful. This all has to mean something. Maybe not for me but for good. Without the Pascal Mystery, this is a meaningless tragedy full of pain. Jesus told us that He is the way and He went to the cross and suffered. But death did not have the last word; He rose from the dead in His body and defeated death for us. He did not defeat suffering. He did not spare any of His loved ones from suffering. Either He enjoys suffering or it has value. It expands you and hopefully does greater good than the pain it causes.

I do believe that suffering expands your very being. With that said, suffering also expands your capacity for joy, as well as, your capacity for love and intimacy. I think that heaven will be sweeter for me and others that suffer greatly because your being is expanded.

In the depths of suffering, feel-good religion falls terribly short. I cannot find peace and comfort from "feel-good" religion. That is wonderful when life is going well, but when you are at the foot of the cross, something deeper is needed. Religion must offer purpose for the pain and the ability to transform your pain. Existentially, life is meaningless when pain enters, and pain is an inevitable part of the human experience. A priest in a concentration camp said, "Only the suffering God can help"[33]. Indeed, God the Son transformed suffering and gave it value so our suffering is not in vain. "[It was the] love of a suffering God that saved the world."[34]

> "All human suffering holds within it a promise of salvation and joy. As Paul has shared in the suffering of Christ, so he is also given a share in Christ's joy. This joy is the fruit of self-sacrificing love, a love so infinite that it has the power to overcome evil. It is the joy of a transcendental purpose that has the capacity to transform our earthly

---

33 Dietrich Bonhoeffer. "AZ Quotes." Accessed November 23, 2016. http://www.chicagomanualofstyle.org/tools_citationguide.html

34 Pope Pius XI. "Caritate Christi Compulsi (On the Sacred Heart)." Accessed November 23, 2016. https://www.ewtn.com/library/ENCYC/P11CARIT.HTM.

suffering from simple resignation or grim endurance into a reason for peace and hope in the glory of eternity."[35]

Behind my veil of sadness is a Christian Hope. "The paradox of the Christian condition which sheds particular light on that of the human condition: neither trials nor sufferings have been eliminated from this world, but they take on a new meaning in the certainty of sharing in the redemption wrought by the Lord and of sharing in His glory. This is why the Christian, though subject to the difficulties of human life, is not reduced to groping for the way; nor does he see in death the end of his hopes."[36]

Darkness allows the illumination of light. The deeper the darkness, the brighter the light. "Joy is the result of a human-divine communion, and aspires to a communion ever more universal." My heart, as the mother of a child with God, is oriented toward the supernatural. "We think of the world of the suffering; we think of all those who have reached the evening of their lives. God's joy is knocking at the door of their physical and moral sufferings, not indeed with irony, but to achieve therein His paradoxical work of transfiguration."[37]

God told Eve, after Original Sin, "I will make your pains in childbearing very severe; with painful labor you will give birth to children."[38]

Genesis is so rich with the "Theology of the Body"[39] and it seems that Genesis 3:16 may show us something about the mercy of God and how He uses evil for good. He uses consequences as a gift to offer something greater. He made childbirth painful and severe, but love comes to life in the process and the child is also a blessing. This consequence of Original Sin is a woman's greatest blessing. The birthing process is painful. Giving birth requires an

---

35 Pope John Paul II, "Salvifici Doloris." Last modified February 11, 1984. https://w2.vatican.va/content/john-paul-ii/en/apost_letters/1984/documents/hf_jp-ii_apl_11021984_salvifici-doloris.html

36 Pope Paul VI. 1975. "Gaudete in Domino." Last modified May 9, 1975. http://w2.vatican.va/content/paul-vi/en/apost_exhortations/documents/hf_p-vi_exh_19750509_gaudete-in-domino.html

37 Ibid.

38 Gen. 3:16.

39 "What is the Theology of the Body?" Theology of the Body, accessed May 31, 2017, http://www.theologyofthebody.net/

expansion of the person. The dilation of the birth canal happens paradoxically through a tightening, a contraction. It seems counterintuitive that through tightening comes expansion, but this seems to be an insight into the Divine Pattern. The Divine Pattern seems to utilize consequences as a means to offer us something greater. The Divine Patten shows that God works in a way that appears so counterintuitive. "My thoughts are nothing like your thoughts," says the LORD. "And my ways are far beyond anything you could imagine."[40]

Our suffering enlarges us and it expands our capacity. It seems this expansion will follow you into eternity because the very being of the person is enlarged. The enlargement dilatasti (Dilatasti: Latin, enlarge) is always a painful process, but the result is much greater than the pain. Giving birth displays that through pain, love comes to life, the child. The suffering of childbirth results in a tremendous blessing of the child. It is a gift. Suffering enlarges you and it produces a larger capacity for eternity. One that suffers enjoys an even greater bliss in heaven. We are all limited by our capacity and we are only able to experience what is within our own limits. God answers our call from our distress. "When I called upon him, the God of my justice heard me: when I was in distress he enlarged me" (Vulg Pss. 4:2).[41]

This is beautiful and offers comfort to realize that suffering in never in vain. The consequence of sin is suffering and death. Jesus conquered death; however, we must go through death to enter eternal life. Death is redeemed, but we still must experience it. What we tend to forget is that suffering too is redeemed. Suffering is used, just as death is used to extrapolate a much greater good. In life, all the wonderful, along with all the terrible and ultimately even death itself is a gift from God.

My Christian joy is derived from Love and I am able to enjoy my other children and my present life. I continue to enjoy Angel, and I look forward to when we are "all in all"[42]. My grief does not rob me of joy. In fact, my very being is expanded, and the joy I feel is more deeply felt because it is a beautiful reprieve from my suffering. Joy and pain are not mutually exclusive, as an emotion, they are one in each of us.

---

40 Isa. 55:8.
41 Ps. 4:2 Vulgate
42 1 Cor. 15:28 New Revised Standard Version Bible: Catholic Edition.

Sister Death

Praised be You, my Lord through Sister Death

—Saint Francis[43]

Angel's first Feast Day—friends and family gathered at her grave

---

43 Saint Francis of Assisi. "Canticle of Brother Sun and Sister Moon of St. Francis of Assisi." Accessed November 24, 2016. http://www.catholic.org/prayers/prayer.php?p=183

R<small>IGHT NOW, MY</small> faith is my only comfort. I cannot imagine this experience without a strong faith. I am also thankful that our faith has the doctrine of the communion of saints that creates solidarity with the dead that is unique. The saints are connected to us in the Body of Christ and this relationship is not postponed. It is active and alive. In fact, we do not believe in death; Angel is resting with Christ. Angel is now part of the Divine and her love is no longer limited by time and space. She was chosen by Him perhaps because she has such a great capacity for love. I can only imagine how many people and animals she is helping throughout the world. It seems that God wants her to share her love beyond her finite human ability. Embodied love is limited by time and space as well as her compassion and generosity. I believe it is true and it is comforting.

Angel was embodied love. She exemplified compassion and generosity. Now, in God, she is part of compassion and generosity. Angel entered into Divine Love.

For me, this isn't just something nice to say, it is my hope. It is the only way I can accept what has happened. I also receive her unlimited love now, and I do not have to wait for my death, to be reunited. Right now, people keep telling me that I keep her in my heart with our memories. I do not believe that she is an abstract memory, she is alive and our relationship is still alive. Our faith does not separate the dead and I am so thankful for this understanding, now it is my lifeline.

The Communion of Saints is my connection to Angel. I look forward to the day when we will be "all in all."[44] I am compelled to visit her resting place because I know that I'm close to her body. I know that she is not separated or limited. Bodily death leads us to greater union. Her body still matters because it is still part of her. Indeed, it is the part of her that is literally part of me. The church respects the remains of its saints, I respect her remains. Just hours after her death a thought entered my mind that she is a Child of the Beatitudes. This thought was not my own, it was given to me.

I shared my letters and feelings of Angel with Father Krys, a family friend, and he said; "I think you are right, the Beatitudes are a part of Angel's and your life. Blessed is SHE, Blessed are you…I think that Jesus gave you these feelings and the Beatitudes passage was read just to ensure you that she is now

---

44 1 Cor. 15:28.

happy in the eternal Love of God, the one who is the Source of Generosity and Compassion."

Jesus does not bring us deliverance from death but deliverance through death. We live in a culture which, in many ways, is death-denying; it is afraid to take a clear look at the fact and the meaning of mortality. Through the death of Jesus, the meaning of death has been changed from the inside. Instead of representing the ultimate separation, it is now the path to greater union. *Yes!* The risen Christ is present now in our midst and gathers a congregation of faith around him to recount the praises of what God has done and to share in a thanksgiving (Eucharistic) meal.

> Communion with the saints. "It is not merely by the title of example that we cherish the memory of those in heaven; we seek, rather, that by this devotion to the exercise of fraternal charity the union of the whole Church in the Spirit may be strengthened. Exactly as Christian communion among our fellow pilgrims brings us closer to Christ, so our communion with the saints joins us to Christ, from whom as from its fountain and head issues all grace, and the life of the People of God itself."[45]

Saint Francis (Angel's Patron Saint) called death, sister death, and this perspective is different. I also think about something I read once about how death is a mercy. It sounds odd, but I realize how true it is. Imagine if this world was the end for us and nothing better was ahead of us. I also think about when I was in Rome and I learned that the dead were buried in what they called "necropolis," meaning places of the dead[46]. Christians changed the burial places to cemeteries because it means—of the sleeping because Christ defeated death. Angel is alive! Sister death gave her eternal life and expanded her Love.

---

45 IntraText Editorial Staff, eds., *Catechism of the Catholic Church.*(Citta del Vaticano: Libreria Editrice Vaticana, 1993), accessed November 11, 2016, http://www.vatican.va/archive/ENG0015/_INDEX.HTM#fonte.
46 "Scavi Tour." Visits to the Tomb of Saint Peter and the Necropolis under the Vatican Basilica, Rome, Italy, September 14th, 2009.

Pope Paul VI wrote about this connection:

All who Belong—to Christ and are in Possession—of His Spirit, combine to make One (1) Church with a Cohesion that depends—on Him (cf. Eph. 4:16). The union of the living with their brethren who have fallen asleep in Christ is not broken; the church has rather believed through the ages that it gains strength from the sharing—of spiritual benefits. The great intimacy of the union of those in heaven with Christ, gives extra steadiness in holiness to the whole church… And makes a manifold contribution to the extension of her building (cf. Cor. 12:12–27). Now that they are welcomed in their own country and at home with the lord (cf. 2 Cor. 5:8), through him, with him and in him, they intercede unremittingly with the Father on our behalf, offering the merit they acquired on earth through Christ Jesus, the one (1) and only mediator between God and man (cf. 1 Tm. 2:5), when they were at god's service in all things, and in their flesh were completing what is lacking—in Christ's afflictions for the sake of his body, the Church (cf. Col. 1:24). Their brotherly care is the greatest help to our weakness."[47]

"I am glad when I suffer for you in my body, for I am participating in the sufferings of Christ that continue for his body, the church."[48]
Suffering, as Saint Francis may express, is our sister because it assists in building the Church. Our suffering may be united with Christ's suffering. This makes our suffering capable of participating in Christ's salvific work. It gives our pain power and it builds up the Church. Perhaps because suffering is an inevitable reality in this life, Christ gave suffering power.

---

47 Pope Paul VI. "Indulgentiarum Doctrina (Apostolic Constitution on Indulgences." Last Modified January 1, 1967. https://www.ewtn.com/library/PAPALDOC/P6INDULG.HTM
48 Col. 1:24.

Faith, When All Feels Hopeless

> There is no doubt that suffering is the greatest trial against our faith; it causes us either to lose it or to strengthen it.
>
> —Gabriele Amorth[49]

I often hear people state God is good after a prayer was answered or after some blessing. Now, I often wonder: would you say God is good if your prayer was not answered? I am speaking of your most heartfelt prayer, your greatest fear realized. The moment when you are on your knees begging God to "let this cup pass"[50], but it doesn't. Then do you say God is good? The goodness of God is easy to see when your life is blessed, but can you see the goodness of God from the darkness? The theological virtue of hope is not fully realized until hope emerges from darkness. Trusting in God when He seems so untrustworthy requires a deep faith that transcends your specific situation.

---

49 Gabriele Amorth, *An Exorcist: More Stories* (San Francisco, CA: Ignatious Press, 2002).
50 Matt. 26:39.

"'Suddenly a great wind came across the desert, struck the four corners of the house, and it fell on the young people, and they are dead; I alone have escaped to tell you.' Then Job arose, tore his robe, shaved his head, and fell on the ground and worshiped. He said, 'Naked I came from my mother's womb, and naked shall I return there; the Lord gave, and the Lord has taken away; blessed be the name of the Lord.'"[51]

Job reveals tremendous faith and love of God. Job's love is not contingent on his blessings. In the end, Job trusted God, but he did not understand all that had happened to him. It is difficult to trust when we know that the just suffer and the wicked prosper (albeit I am both wicked and just). The Kingdom of God does not reign here on earth; therefore, we cannot limit God's goodness to this life alone.

Can God be trusted in the most tragic situation? Is He good? In His omnipotence, He allows horrific things to happen to people who do not deserve so much pain. This is why many people do not believe in God or in God's goodness. When tragedy strikes, God is with you in all His goodness, with His love and grace.

I emphatically believe that God's plan is unfolding and His Providence is working toward a greater glory. "For surely I know the plans I have for you, says the Lord, plans for your welfare and not for harm, to give you a future with hope."[52] God has plans for Angel and all His children, "not for harm."[53] Death was defeated by Christ and this is the foundation of our Christian belief. Through Christ, we partake in the Divine life and this end is the purpose of everything. I know that Angel lives in Christ and she is doing His will.

Jesus showed us "the way"[54] and He went to the cross, He suffered and He died. Death was conquered through the cross. The worst thing in hu-

---

51 Job 1:19–21.
52 Jer. 29:11.
53 Ibid
54 John 14:6.

man history became the greatest thing in human history, the cross. Christ makes all things new. In giving we receive, in helplessness power, in humility we receive glory and in dying we receive eternal life. Sometimes when God seems the opposite of good, he is working through suffering for greater glory.

Easter is not possible without Good Friday. Holy Friday or Good Friday seems counterintuitive, but we know Good Friday is a gift. Mary, His mother, deeply suffered through Good Friday. I am sure it was the worst day of her life. We know that Jesus suffered a gruesome death, yet we still dare to call it Holy Friday. The saint's feast days, the day they died, are a celebration. Suffering and death are celebrated. We need to remember that we celebrate death because death is the birth of eternal life.

It seems to me that many Christians, myself included, want to celebrate Easter without Good Friday. Perhaps ignoring Good Friday is the reason we expect blessings from God and perceive that all suffering is bad. Celebrating Easter without Good Friday leads to an understanding that expects joy without pain and the pattern of life always has both. Many people lose faith because Easter is expected without Holy Friday and nothing is good about their own suffering. He is the way and He transforms everything and makes all things good.

All things pass in this life. We are all dying. Many, especially in the west, want to deny death. Death is so negative! Saint Francis called death his sister. He understands that God is working everything toward good. Often, when heaven directly communicated with a person on earth it started with "do not be afraid."[55] This is not a promise that you will not suffer. I think this is the point that is often lost. "Be not afraid"[56] (Gen. 45:5 Douay Version) means to trust that our Lord is making all things new. Nothing that happens is in vain. We can trust Him in the midst of tragedy because He will use it for good. Everything belongs and our Lord, our friend and brother, is unfolding His plan for the good.

---

55 Gen. 15:1.
56 Gen. 45:5 Douay Version

Pope Francis explains that difficulties and suffering are the same journey as Christ. Jesus says that those who follow Him will have "many good things" but "with persecution."⁵⁷ The path of the Lord, he continued, "is a road of humility, a road that ends in the Cross." That is why, he added, "there will always be difficulties," "persecution." There will always be, "because He travelled this road before" us. The Pope warned that "when a Christian has no difficulties in life—when everything is fine, everything is beautiful—something is wrong." It leads us to think that he or she is "a great friend of the spirit of the world, of worldliness." The Pope noted this "is a temptation particular to Christians." "Following Jesus is just that: going with Him out of love, behind Him: on the same journey, the same path. And the spirit of the world will not tolerate this and what will make us suffer, but suffering as Jesus did. Let us ask for this grace: to follow Jesus in the way that He has revealed to us and that He has taught us. This is beautiful, because he never leaves us alone. Never! He is always with us. So be it."⁵⁸

---

57 Jesus Caritas. "Pope Francis 'To Follow Jesus in the Way' and the Latest from Vatican." Last modified May 29, 2013. http://jceworld.blogspot.com/2013/05/pope-francis-to-follow-jesus-in-way-and.html

58 Ibid

Abandonment Draws Us Closer to Christ

My God, my God, why have you forsaken me?[59]

—Matthew 27:46

Prescious

---

59 Matt. 27:46 New Revised Standard Version Bible: Catholic Edition.

THE FEELING OF abandonment by God is most acutely experienced when you trust God and your request is rejected. When you put your trust in God and He lets you down. When you are on your knees begging God to "let this cup pass"[60] and it does not. That's the moment when you feel most abandoned by God. When God allows your greatest fear to become a reality. From that perspective, He seems untrustworthy and even undesirable.

I now realize that the feeling of abandonment by God is derived from a deep faith in God and his goodness. One does not feel abandoned by nothing or one that is not trusted for his or her goodness. Abandonment's prerequisites are trust and the expectation of a magnanimously good God. It seems that many believe that faith is derived from blind trust and that is a form of faith. In my Dark Night I realized that my faith is deep and in my disappointment of God is the exact place that I found Him, but I am still on my journey.

Fulton Sheen in the *Cross and the Beatitudes* states: "The night of the agony in the garden when that atonement for pride began in all horror, he described his soul as 'sorrowful unto death'; and now on the cross he lives the Beatitude of the Poor in Spirit by proclaiming the last and greatest poverty of all—the spiritual poverty of seeming abandonment by God." Sheen articulates the holiness of feeling abandoned: "so abandonment is felt not by the ungodly and unholy, but by the most holy of men, Our Lord on the Cross."[61]

The truth is that I was angry with God and I need to be honest about that. It feels like He knew what would hurt me the most and that didn't matter. I have logically worked out many reasons, but it doesn't change how I felt. I feared God and sometimes I didn't know how to love Him, I don't know that I ever knew. Who is He? Now I realize that I deeply resented Him after the accident. I logically believed God is good, but I didn't always feel that He is good. He felt like a bully that breaks those He loves. I know that God is good and loving, but I greatly feared that He is an untrustworthy bully. I understand that our beautiful Lord became incarnate to show us the love of the Father. I know He is Love, but I do not always feel His love. Sometimes I think my fear is that God is just, and I deserve all this suffering, but I know

---

60 Matt. 26:39.
61 Fulton J. Sheen, *The Cross and the Beatitudes* (Tacoma: Angelico Press, 2012), 41.

that a loving God does not send this kind of suffering as a lesson. A god that would do that is not the God who is Love. Jesus became incarnate to show us His Father's Love in the flesh, and His Love is beautiful and perfect. I know my fears and feelings are not reflective of who God really is.

I believe that part of my anger with God is derived from my trust and love of Him. I feel as if He has been unfaithful to me. It feels like infidelity, a broken relationship. This is a very personal response that must be articulated and given a voice. God let me down, and sometimes I don't know how to pick up the pieces. I try to remember that God has the ability to heal our relationship because I am unable to myself. *"A bruised reed he will not break, and a dimly burning wick he will not quench; he will faithfully bring forth justice."* [62]

I must give God my heartfelt anger and "Be still and know that I am God."[63] When we spiritually suffer, we feel abandoned because spiritual suffering feels contrary to good. In the experience of feeling abandoned, we are united to Christ who cries out, "My God, my God, why have you forsaken me?"[64] Jesus, quoting a lament Psalm, seems to be having a very natural human experience of feeling abandoned in His suffering. Even God the Son felt abandoned because He went through the entire human experience to save us. In suffering, especially in suffering, He humbled Himself and His experience of feeling abandoned displays the feelings of abandonment which are used for our edification. As always, God uses it for good.

Through my reflections I realize how much God loves me. Sometimes the brutality of His love is beautiful. Jesus, the Logos/Sarx,(Logos—the Word of God, or principle of divine reason and creative order, identified in the Gospel of John with the second person of the Trinity incarnate in Jesus Christ; Sarx—Greek for flesh/body)[65] hung on the Tree of Life in unimaginable agony and felt the very human experience of feeling abandoned by God. It was the great

---

62 Isa. 42:3.
63 Ps. 46:10.
64 Mark 15:34.
65 *Bible Gateway* Blog. https://www.biblegateway.com/blog/2014/12/the-logos-became-sarx/

crescendo of his kenosis (Greek for emptying).⁶⁶ Jesus felt abandoned by God and gave salvific power to this very human experience. It must be noted that as Jesus looked heavenward for His Father, at His feet, was His mother. She was present and her relationship with her son was perhaps at its closest point in His feeling of abandonment. She was faithful and steadfast; she was there for Him in His darkest hour. Most mothers are not present for their children when they are between this life and the next; as a mother it is indeed your most difficult hour. As a mother, the pain it caused is worth enduring for the sake of your child. I was Mary; I was present, to pray and to kiss her feet. In the feeling of abandonment Mary is always your companion.

Right now, I live in Holy Saturday awaiting the fruits of the Resurrection. I'm living in Holy Saturday and this makes my earnest desire for Easter much greater. On Holy Saturday Christ descended into Hell. God became separated from God and mother separated from her Son. The "one in being with the father"⁶⁷ felt God forsakenness. Christ feels the full loss of the Father because He was in perfect communion with Him. "My God my God, why have you forsaken me?"⁶⁸ The lament gives voice to the depths of feeling abandoned and despair. It displays the genuine struggle that faith must endure to enter into a deeper relationship with God: A relationship that requires suffering and surrender. It requires a submission that feels unsafe and insecure. The faith of a child is unquestioning and pure and it is very good. In time, an authentic faith must go into darkness, the dark night.

Knowing that Jesus had the comfort of His mother helps. When I've felt abandoned by God in my grief, I never felt abandoned by Mary. I know that she will always bring her children to her Son. When God seems far, she never feels distant. She is not God and that is partially her appeal. She is not in

---

66 "Kenosis," Theopedia, accessed June 29, 2017, http://www.theopedia.com/kenosis
67 David Bennet. "The Nicene Creed: Symbol of the Catholic Faith." Last modified April 1, 2016. http://www.ancient-future.net/nicene.html
68 Ps. 22:1.

control, so all she can do is accompany you. She is the perfect disciple and example of surrender; Fiat (Latin—let it be done) is her only answer to God[69].

What do I believe? I believe that we are created in God's image and this requires a certain subjectivity that is immortal from the moment of creation. In each of us, God gave immense dignity. He gave us a body and soul to make the person. From the moment of creation, every person is immortal and seeks full union. Union is heaven. Love always seeks greater union and heaven is the fulfillment of being in communion. Abandonment leads to greater Communion.

---

[69] Joe Reciniello. "Mary's 'Yes' is Called the Fiat: In Latin, "Let It Be Done." Last modified April 4, 2016, http://www.catholic365.com/article/4008/marys-yes-is-called-the-fiat-in-latin-let-it-be-done.html

My God is a God of the Living

> He is not the God of the dead, but of the
> living, for to him all are alive.
>
> —Mark 12:27[70]

The language and gestures of Christians about a person who has passed into the next life greatly implies that the person ceased to exist. After my daughter entered eternity, I felt scandalized by the way my fellow Christians spoke of death. I thought we believe that Christ defeated death; however, fellow Christians thought it was proper to begin the process of erasing her existence. As if she is no more. On the first Christmas most people left her name off our Christmas greetings, as if she is no longer a part of my family. (I realize that people did not mean to be hurtful.) People state that she was "a good person" or "was nice" and so on. She is still as wonderful as before. When I speak of her and use present tense language, people get uncomfortable. When I am talking about a specific moment in time, I use past tense language, but if I am talking about her, I use present tense. Some seem to think that I am denying her entrance into eternal life. I am acutely aware that my Angel is no longer in

[handwritten annotation: Yes — "my husband..."]

---
70 Mark 12:27.

her mortal life, but she is still Angel. She moved into eternity. She is still fully alive and more deeply a part of the Communion of Saints.

My God is God of the living. Scripture emphasizes this point—"Now he is God not of the dead, but of the living; for to him all of them are alive." [71] It is our hope, yet we continue to speak of "the dead." I believe that Christ defeated death for us, and we move through death into everlasting life. This is a tenet of our Faith, yet our language and gestures demonstrate the contrary. Death takes a person out of time and releases us from the limitations that time and space put on our mortal existence. Perhaps the proper perspective is to recognize that they are outside of linear time. Does this mean that they do not have a future? In terms of linear time and space their future is over or complete, but Angel's existence still is and I constantly implore her for help and prayers. If she exists and she is active, she has a future in a manner of existence; although, a future devoid of time. This is a paradox as many religious truths seem to be. Angel continues to bless my life through her existence, which is still loving and beautiful. Indeed, our love is stronger than death. "Set me as a seal upon your heart, as a seal upon your arm; for love is strong as death, passion fierce as the grave."[72] John, Angel's big brother, has Angel tattooed forever on his arm. On the inside of his arm it states, "Song 8:6" because his love for her is stronger than death. My family cherishes our sweet Angel and our love for her is indeed stronger than death.

Angel is a child of the Beatitudes. Angel is kind and beautiful. Angel is a person who loves with all her being. Angel is humorous and fun. Angel is compassionate and generous. Angel is my daughter, my saint.

---

71 Luke 20:38.
72 Song of Sol. 8:6.

The death of a dear one requires that you continue to love, even though there is nothing tangible. I believe this is why Jesus left access to His body in the Real Presence. Thankfully, this gives access to Angel too. Angel's body continues to matter, even after this earthly life because I treasure everything that was hers. I continue to love Angel as a person, a body/soul. A memory is not what I love, I love a person; I love Angel. She is more than a memory! With our Resurrected bodies, I will hug her body again with mine; I will kiss her lips again with my lips. I earnestly believe this with the great theological virtues: faith, hope, and love.

A friend sent me a link to a beautiful story in Mount Lady of Carmel of Varroville Parish bulletin. This perspective displays a God of the Living Communion of Saints.

> The union of the saints in heaven with us in the Eucharist is expressed in a delightful story about a parish priest on a small Greek island in the Aegean Sea. One day a visitor asked the pastor, "How many people usually worship here on Sunday?" The priest's answer was, "Oh, about ten to twelve thousand, I would suppose." The visitor was somewhat bewildered. "This is a tiny island," she said, "and the church is small. Where do all these people come from and how can they possibly fit into so small a church building?" The priest smiled and then said to the visitor, "All the people who ever lived on this island since it received the gospel message are still here. Just think of what we say in the sacred liturgy: 'Therefore with all the angels and the saints and the whole company of the faithful we praise your glory forever.' Don't you realize," he added, "that when we sing the Trisagion (Holy, Holy, Holy) we are joining with all the holy ones who have ever worshiped in this church?" How appropriate it is for us to be aware that when we gather to celebrate the Eucharist many more are present and active than mortal vision is able to see. It is worth noting too that it is not they who join us, but we who join them. We and the saints are related as friends, especially friends around the altar, but also friends in carrying on the unfinished tasks which they left to us." [73]

---

[73] "Our Lady of Mount Carmel Parish," last modified October 28th, 2012, http://www.olmcvarroville.org.au/images/Bulletins/2012/Bulletin_28th_October_2012.pub.pdf

Pilgrimage to Calvary

> For it is in faith that we journey, not in clear vision, and what we shall be has not yet been manifested. The New Jerusalem, of which we are already citizens, and sons and daughters, comes down from above, from God. Of this only lasting city we have not yet contemplated the splendor, except as in a mirror and in a confused way, by holding fast to the prophetic word. But already we are its citizens, or we are invited to become so; every spiritual pilgrimage receives its interior meaning from its ultimate destination.
>
> —Pope Paul VI[74]

It is difficult to express the level of pain that every anniversary or event brings. To miss her first birthday, Christmas, Homecoming, and the list goes on and on. I knew that the first year anniversary of her walk into eternity was going to be intensely difficult. I decided to celebrate Angel's first Feast Day by traveling to where eternal life began. My sister and I made a pilgrimage to Israel because it was so important for me to focus on Angel's life after

---

[74] Pope Paul VI, "Gaudete in Domino," Last modified May 9, 1975. http://w2.vatican.va/content/paul-vi/en/apost_exhortations/documents/hf_p-vi_exh_19750509_gaudete-in-domino.html

death. I knew that if I do not put her immortality at the center of my focus, I would fall into depression and despair. Being on pilgrimage allowed me to literally immerse myself, body and soul, in my faith.

We made the Via Dolorosa. Via Dolorosa (Way of Grief) is a road in the old city of Jerusalem, a path where Jesus was lead in agony, carrying the crucifixion cross. The Franciscan monks walk the "way of the cross" every Friday at 3:00 p.m.[75] Every Friday they literally walk the way of Jesus to the place of His crucifixion[76]. It is the Stations of the Cross on the actual place that it is believed to have happened. I walked the way of the cross with the Franciscans; I walked with Christ to the cross.

Calvary is marked by the Church of the Holy Sepulchre in Jerusalem. Being at Calvary made me feel so close to the Virgin. I was standing with her at the "foot of the cross."[77] Death lost its power and I wanted my entire being to stand against the defeat of death. When I saw death's power on my beloved child, I earnestly desired to see death's defeat.

---

75 "Walking in the Footsteps of Christ," Catholic Diocese of Little Rock, accessed June 21, 2017, https://www.dolr.org/stations-of-the-cross/jerusalem
77 John 19:25.

AN ANGEL OF THE BEATITUDES

The Mount of the Beatitudes

I also deeply desired to see the Mount of the Beatitudes, but I had no idea that it is the most beautiful place in Israel! It's heaven on earth! It is so lush and vibrant, like an oasis in the dessert. Naomi and I were there on September 16 and I had no idea how edifying it was just to be there. On the Mount of the Beatitudes there is a tree that had people's names etched on it. I put Angel's name on it and now Angel's name is forever etched in a tree on the

Mount of the Beatitudes. My Child of the Beatitudes was present in all her love. On the Mount of the Beatitudes there is a Church that marks the spot where Jesus preached the Sermon on the Mount: "And seeing the multitude he went up into a mountain…and he opened his mouth and taught them."[78] Unsurprisingly, it's a Franciscan church. I knew that Angel led me there, and I even had a wonderful dream about her that night (Angel often visits me in my dreams). My pilgrimage was full of blessings and grace.

---

78 Matt. 5:1–2.

Beyond the Language of the Living

My Angel, my Joy Baby, was spared great suffering. She died without pain and her life was protected from difficult pain. She was innocent and unharmed. Perhaps God knew that her heart could not withstand the suffering of this world. She suffered with people; she has immense compassion. God's Providence allowed Angel to enter eternity before she had to suffer. This is how she serves the divine economy. God has a path for us all. My other children are as special as Angel and they are as dear to me as she is. God wants them to serve Him and humanity in this life.

After the loss, the greatest of losses, I go to her resting place and the terrible silence haunts me. Sometimes it feels that my love has no object. I feel alone in silence. Suddenly words of Hope permeate my soul through the words of T.S. Elliot: "They can tell you, being dead: the communication of the dead is tongued with fire beyond the language of the living."[79] Perhaps the silence is not silence at all? Perhaps the language is "beyond the living" and if only we could hear it. I do not hear a dog whistle, yet it is not silent[80]. Maybe my sweet Love is always talking to me in a language that I am unable to hear. Perhaps in the depths of my soul, I can sometimes hear her. Baby, along with all the angels and saints, has a voice that is "tongued with fire." [81]Perhaps, this is the language of the Word. This language is part of the very life of God that surrounds us. *Yes*

---

79 T.S. Eliot, *Four Quartets* (New York: Harcourt Brace & Company, 1943), 96-116.
80 Ibid.
81 Ibid.

Pope Benedict XVI comforted me in his book, *The Joy of Knowing Christ*. The Pope masterfully articulates how Jesus is with us now in this life.

So what does the Feast of the Ascension of the Lord mean for us? It does not mean that the Lord has departed to some place far from people and from the world. Christ's Ascension is not a journey into space toward the most remote stars; for basically, the planets, like the earth, are also made of physical elements.

Christ's Ascension means that he no longer belongs to the world of corruption and death that condition our lives. It means that he belongs entirely to God. He, the Eternal Son, led our human existence into God's presence, taking with him flesh and blood in a transfigured form.

The human being finds room in God; through Christ, the human being was introduced into the very life of God. And since God embraces and sustains the entire cosmos, the Ascension of the Lord means that Christ has not departed from us, but that He is now, thanks to His being with the Father, close to each one of us forever. Each one of us can be on intimate terms with Him; each can call upon Him.[82]

Perhaps Christ's Ascension into heaven was not a departure from this earth, but an assimilation for us into the very life of God. The life of God is not contained by space or time. It is a mystery that surrounds us and, thanks to Christ, we are part of this mysterious life of God. The language that is "tonged with fire" surpasses us so we do not hear it. The Words affect us and the life of God is not separated from us because, in Him, we are part of it.

---

[82] Pope Benedict XVI, *The Joy of Knowing Christ: Meditations on the Gospels* (Frederick, Maryland: The Word Among Us Press, 2009) 138.

ANAMNESIS

My joyful memories of Angel became very painful. I'd remember her and feel a great emptiness and loss. The most joyful moments in my life became a source of pain. I realized that past moments of joy, derived from the virtue of love, remain joyful. The beautiful memories of all my children are a part of my love and the love inside me is the immortal part of me. Joy is eternal. When joy becomes painful it is helpful to realize that the joy still exists, like Angel, the joy still is.

Anamnesis is a term that I read about years ago, yet it stayed with me. It means so much more than "remembrance" (anamnesis- Greek calling to mind, recollection).[83] The Jews celebrated Passover and made present for every passing generation. Our emphasis on remembrance is intrinsically related to our nature that needs to symbolize and recognize eternal truth. Our remembrance is not for the sake of recollection; it's a renewal.

After the consecration at Mass, the prayer of remembrance comes in which the Church calls to mind the Lord's passion, resurrection, and ascension into heaven. This is the high point of the Mass as a memorial of what occurred during Christ's visible stay on earth as a pledge of what he continues to do invisibly through the Eucharist.

When the church remembers the sacrifice of Christ in the Eucharist, they are recalling it not only to mind, but also to present effect. Remembrance

---

83 Henry George Liddell and Robert Scott., *A Greek-English Lexicon*, trans. Sir Henry Stuart Jones (Oxford: Clarendon Press, 1940), accessed June 21, 2017, http://www.perseus.tufts.edu/hopper/text?doc=Perseus%3Atext%3A1999.04.0057%3Aentry%3Da) na%2Fmnhsis

brings the effects of a past event to bear on the present. It identifies one directly with those people for whom that past event was a present reality.

I continue to make Angel present through my memories and dreams. I also have a keen awareness of her presence in the Eucharist. She is united to God and when I receive Him, I receive her. She becomes present. I hold on to my memories and recall every gesture and mannerism. I do this to make her present, not just to remember her. It is the difference between remembrance and anamnesis. To recall the past allows a memory to be fostered. Anamnesis is remembering and making her present. It seems this is possible because we do this in the Eucharist. I utilize anamnesis to keep her active and really present in my life, not through a religious ritual but through heartfelt memories. I constantly talk to her and she continues to inspire me. I love her dearly, and I know that she is fully alive in eternity, so my love has an object, a person—Angel.

Jesus is "the way, and the truth, and the life."[84] The Word became flesh and dwelt among us. The Word or Logos can be translated as the Wisdom of God became flesh. God was wholly divine and wholly human. Why was this necessary? God Himself entered into our human condition to save us from death. Sin hurts our relationship with the Holy One and it creates a division. Man, in various ways and through all cultures, has attempted to repair that relationship with sacrifice. It seems this inclination stems from a desire for justice. Jesus gave Himself and He is the only sacrifice that is worthy of repairing our relationship with God. In the sacrifice of His Body, it is offered to God and the people of God, to share. In the "breaking of the bread"[85] Jesus returns to us and we consume His body to become one with Him and the entire Body of Christ. It is our great thanksgiving; it is our sacrifice.

Angel is alive and now I can still be close to her, even though her body is not here. In God, we unite and become one in Him. This does not happen later, it happens now! Not all things are confined to time. Faith, hope, and love are eternal because God is their source. A mother's joyful memories of her children are a resonation of Trinitarian Love.

---

84 John 14:6
85 Luke 24:35.

Heaven at the Center

> The ultimate reason Christ has come is not merely to heal the deficiencies and diseases of this earthly life. He comes also because there is an even greater sickness and suffering that we all share: the possibility of a life eternally separated from God. Christ has come to restore the most fundamental and devastating disease of humanity: the loss of eternal life. (separation)
>
> —Pope John Paul II[86]

I know that Angel is outside of time: with God in the eternal now. The eternal now is not "waiting" for a future event. That would put God inside of time, we are the ones waiting. Angel is not waiting for us; she already has me and the rest of my family. In fact, she is in full communion with us so she has us more than ever before. I find great comfort in that thought. I also believe that when I take His body and eat it, I am so close to her.

In the medieval theory of geocentrism, earth was believed to be the center of the universe. From our perspective, earth is still the center and everything. It appears that everything else revolves around it, including God.

---

[86] Pope John Paul II, "Salvifici Doloris." Last modified February 11, 1984. https://w2.vatican.va/content/john-paul-ii/en/apost_letters/1984/documents/hf_jp-ii_apl_11021984_salvifici-doloris.html

As a bereaved Christian mother, I realized that I am stuck in a spiritual Geocentricism that does not really value life beyond earth as a meaningful life. The Christian faith gives us the proper language to value our lives in heaven, but it does not resonate through how we perceive life beyond death as a life with purpose. All Christians know that heaven is our ultimate destiny, and all pain and suffering will end, and we will live in the presence of God. All Christians want to go to heaven to be with God and see their loved ones and suffer no more. If we are honest, we will realize that heaven is not really "valued" except as a place to have our desires fulfilled. Many faithful Christians would avoid ever leaving this world if they had a choice. This has implications, even if unintended. It implies that life in heaven is not really desirable, even though we say it is.

It is important to recognize this inconsistency so we can grow in a more mature understanding that aligns with what we already know to be true. When someone says to a bereaved person that his or her loved one is in a better place, does he or she really mean it? Death is difficult because our earthly life lacks the fullness of heaven. I think we want to believe it, but lack a "heaven-centric" perspective that supports the basic tenets of our Christian faith. A heaven-centric foundation that the first Christians clearly had is witnessed by the many martyrs of the early church. A person willing to die for God is a person who really believes that heaven is invaluable and heaven is truly a "better place." I believe that a heaven-centric perspective cannot devalue earthly life because it has meaning and value too. Both are important and heaven is the fulfillment and union of our earthly life.

My Angel left this world for the next at age fifteen. She did not have the opportunity to live a long, productive life. She will never grow up. She will never graduate from high school or college. She will never get married, have a career, or be a mother. Angel was gifted, beautiful, kind, and generous. Indeed, she had so much to offer this world. Why do I feel like all this is now wasted? She will not enjoy many of the gifts of this life; however, I realized that this does not mean that her life in heaven is not gifted. Clearly, understanding life in heaven is beyond our finite, limited world view, but it seems to be devalued by even the best-intentioned Christians. Perhaps it is because we perceive that it lacks many gifts of this world. Perhaps it is because we are so repelled by death. Maybe because death was not originally intended for humanity, so we cannot fully appreciate how death was defeated by Christ. Perhaps it is simply devalued because it is unknown.

I believe that all life has immense meaning on its own terms. A meaningful life in heaven is surely related to this life, but it is much, much more. I believe heaven reconciles all divisions, especially heaven and earth. We are made for love. Every good on earth is secondary to love. We are made to give and receive love. Like the Trinity, we are made for full union, perfect relationships. Angel's life in heaven is not wasted!

For too long we have made God an object of desire. Do we love God for love of God, or do we just want Him to quench our many desires? We put God into our little selves without realizing His glory that is far beyond our comprehension. It seems that petition prayer is the most common form of prayer. How much of your personal prayer time is petitioning for yourself? Petitioning for others is a form of love. Do you talk to God about your life? Do you just tell him things that you would tell your lover or most intimate friend? Most of my prayer time is a conversation, and now Angel is included in my conversation with God. God and of course Angel are not tools of my desires. They are my intimate lovers.

Ilia Delio has explained, "For too long we have made God an object of our desire, hope, frustration, and anger. But God is not an object outside ourselves onto which we can project what is within ourselves."[87] This makes God in man's image. Man/woman becomes the central point and this skews our ability to know God and love Him for who He is. I think that it is very difficult to truly love God when man/woman is at the center.

All goods on earth are leading us to the good. Sometimes it feels as if Angel is missing so much good. I try to remind myself that all goods that I know are a foretaste of the good that she knows. She is not "missing out" on anything. She is in the fullness of life with all true goodness.

---

87 Ilia Delio, *Compassion: Living in the Spirit of Saint Francis* (New York: Franciscan Media, 2011), 15.

I've always told my children that heaven is not a place to have your desires fulfilled (in an earthly sense of desire). Heaven is about God, about union and love. I never wanted them to think that heaven was about something selfish because heaven is much greater than any earthly desire, greater than you. Heaven is the perfect exchange of love. Every earthly desire is actually derived from a desire of God. This is what makes heaven, heaven; union with God and each other. I believe the desire we have now becomes so miniscule because our true desire will be fulfilled. *desires in alignment with God's will — the Lord's prayer.*

I remember Angel told me that some kids at school were talking about heaven and they stated that they will be able to eat what they want and do whatever they wanted. Angel expressed that she disagreed because she knew that heaven is much greater than that. She didn't say anything to them, but she knew heaven as something greater than us. I'm thankful that she understood this before her entrance into love. Of course, I agree that heaven will be blissful and I'm sure many lesser goods here on earth may be enjoyed in heaven. I believe it is important to realize that heaven is not for you, but that you are for heaven. *Wow!*

I need to stay connected to my dear Angel. If the connection is severed, all of my hope is lost and everything I believe is in vain. For me, after the bodily death of a child, the world became a very different place. The only things that really matter are the transcendent and you see how foolish we are about things that do not matter at all. I believe this is a gift of the permanent condition of bereaved parents. The only things that matter is what really matters. Life is not wasted and heaven is valued. Indeed, part of me is already in heaven. *Yes :)*

My brother wrote us a beautiful letter within hours of the accident. I kept a copy of it with me for the first year after the accident because it was such a comfort. My brother uses metaphorical language to give voice to the extraordinary love, innocence, and joy that Angel displayed. Of course, Angel is not an angel, but he uses her name to convey her "saintly spirit."

Emily and Ward,
    Until now, I did not realize that Angel was the perfect name for her. Christina is fond of telling our children they were once angels

the biggest part of you :)

AN ANGEL OF THE BEATITUDES

in heaven and God gave us a precious gift with each of their births. She says they slipped the bonds of heaven to be with us. But, Angel was different in that she never severed her heavenly ties. Her feet never quite touched the earth. She maintained her spiritual bond with heaven. Her soul was filled with so much love it was as if she was not of this world—a world filled with hate and cruelty. Most people lose their innocence, will grow cynical and jaded, and let slip their heavenly ties. This world bombards our children with sin and despair until they lose the grace and spirit that once filled their souls in heaven. Angel was impervious to the darkness that surrounds our world. She never let go of her heavenly grace.

Angel was too good for this world and many of us were undeserving of the light she brought to our lives. So, she went back to where she belongs, among the host of angels. Angel is now at peace where she belongs. We are left here but our lives have been made richer by her love and her saintly spirit. We must be thankful for the joy she brought, and the slice of heaven she brought to our lives.

As we grow old, she will remain young. In twenty, forty, even one hundred years, she will never grow old. She will never grow weary of this cruel world. She will never lose her innocence. She will remain forever young and eternally pure. This is part of the gift that God has given us. So we must be thankful for the joy she brought us and the love she shared with us. And we should recognize the miracle that she was—a soul that came down from heaven and never stopped being an angel.

Love,
Uncle John

The Gift, Communion

Jesus said, "That they all shall be one, just as you, my Father, are in me, and I am in you, so that they also shall be one in us."

—John 17:21[88]

Everything is leading us to communion, even death. Angel has fallen asleep in Christ, and I am still connected to her in Him. I know that love always seeks greater union. My relationship with her is not postponed until the next life. Now, the good news is not about doing it right to get to heaven. It is about love; it is about union. A love that is life-giving and derived from grace. Angel understands that love means union. That is why she always tried to include the excluded. "The curtain of the temple was torn in two, from top to bottom"[89] when Christ died. The divine is no longer separated. The temple displayed how God and man/woman are separated; therefore, when Christ died the curtain of separation was "torn in two."[90] I used to think holiness is separated from un-holiness. Christ made all things new and reconciled everything, even evil. Only God can do that.

---

88 John 17:21.
89 Mark 15:38.
90 Ibid.

AN ANGEL OF THE BEATITUDES

I used to be most concerned about rules [the law] and worthiness and not about relationship. Really, I wanted to be in control and not in a relationship with my Father. I did not realize that none of us are worthy and we all need a savior that gives us His saving grace. It's a gift and it is beyond my control of my own worthiness. Like many great mysteries, it's a paradox. Acknowledgement of our unworthiness makes us worthy. God is almost always showing us paradox, and I believe that is because He makes everything new. The real truth is that everything belongs, the good and the bad in life. All the pain and joy, all the love and anger—*everything*! You see, this is what it means when Jesus said He makes all things new. He really does. In giving we receive, in helplessness power, in humility we receive glory, and in dying we receive eternal life. The worst thing in human history became the greatest thing in human history—the cross. It's always in paradox and our lives work the same way. Everything is gift, even the hard things.

Father Richard Rohr explains how everything belongs, "God can be found in all things, even and most especially in the painful, tragic, and sinful things, exactly where we do not want to look for God."[91] [Wow]

---

91 Richard Rohr, *Everything Belongs, the Gift of Contemplative Prayer*, (New York: Crossroad Publishing Company, 2003), 177.

The Problem of Transformation

In the beginning of my grief I did not want to accept that anything good could ever come from this tragedy. To me, that seemed to "justify" what happened. It seemed as if that would make her death "worth it" and I didn't want any part of that. Only as a slow process was I able to even fathom good coming from losing her. I feel that I must address this because it was a drastic feat that I had to overcome.

A grief counselor once said this about the death of her husband and child; she asserted that God wanted her to want Him more than she wanted her husband and child. I was repelled by the statement because it seemed to imply that God took them to teach her He is more important. She may not have meant that at all, but that's how I heard it.

I realize that we are called to love God first, but I believe we do that through our love of other people as well. Loving God and loving neighbors are not mutually exclusive, they are intermingled. I do not believe that God is offended by the unfailing love of a mother; in fact I believe He finds joy in it. It is not a contest of winners and losers. "God is Love"[92] and that includes a mother's love for her child. <u>It is a holy love that builds up the Kingdom of God.</u> Yes

A god that will take a child and husband to show that He is most important is a god of jealousy and spite. I believe we tend to make ourselves the center of everything, including the death of a loved one. Our concupiscence makes us view the world from our selfish viewpoint. Everything is not

---

92 1 John 4:8.

exclusively about you. For me, realizing this is helpful because it alleviated some of my guilt. Did God do this to punish me? Did this happen because I was not as careful as I should be as a mother? The list goes on and on...This kind of guilt is often derived from a sense of egocentrism. Deep down, we all really think we are in control; that we are God.

My God of love took Angel into eternity and placed her in the very life of God. For reasons that I will not know in this life, but I am now able to trust that God is using it for good. I no longer feel that I am cooperating with her death to realize that God is transforming all of this into good; <u>in fact, he is transforming it into love.</u>

The City of Perry named a Dog Park after Angel because of her great love for animals. The outpouring of love from our community displays great love and the manifestation of transforming suffering.

"Why not me?"

(Jesus) did *not announce for a future society the reign of an ideal happiness from which suffering would be banished; but, by His lessons and by His example, He traced the path of the happiness which is possible on earth and of perfect happiness in Heaven: the royal way of the Cross.*

—Pope Pius X[93]

Arthur Ashe was a victim of AIDS that he contracted through a blood transfusion. Ashe understood that blessings and evil may enter any of our lives. He wisely answered his own lament—why? "If I were to say, 'God, why me' about the bad things, then I should have said, 'God, why me' about the good things that happened in my life."[94] Ashe understands that blessings and hardship enter our lives, but God should be trusted in all things. The question then becomes inverted, why not me? This resonated with me because of the humble truth in the answer. I realized that suffering is a part of the human condition, and if any member of the human family suffers, none of us are

---

93 Pope Pius X. "Notre Charge Apostolique." Accessed November 14, 2016. http://www.chicagomanualofstyle.org/tools_citationguide.html

94 Arthur Ashe. "Arthur Ashe Quotes." Accessed November 14, 2016 https://www.brainyquote.com/quotes/authors/a/arthur_ashe.html

above it. None of us are protected from it, albeit suffering occurs on various levels. God loves all of His children so one should never feel like they are more important to God than another. As if one "deserves" suffering and the other doesn't. Suffering is a mystery which we are all subjected to. "Why not me" is the humble response that answers the terrible question of "Why?"

Job, the just man, suffered.[95] This is the monotheistic dilemma because terrible things happen and we have only one good God. Polytheistic religion attributed evil to one god and good to another, monotheistic religion must reconcile suffering with a good god. Suffering and death entered the human condition with sin; however, Christ gave suffering power through the cross.

I was talking with a woman around the time of a presidential election, and she stated that she was not worried about the election because God will protect our country. I immediately knew that I disagreed on a certain level because not all countries are "protected." To me, saying that implies that God does not care about countries that suffer extreme civil unrest, or poverty, or even genocide. Does God protect some and leave others to suffer? Do we think that God does not choose to protect little children who have a horrific illness or physical abuse? I do believe that God is with the suffering, but we are not "protected" from suffering. The kingdom of God is not the ushering of a kingdom without suffering. In fact, the kingdom of God requires suffering.

I am not at all saying that we should not trust in God, on the contrary, we must trust more deeply in God. Many believers are disappointed in God when something terrible happens because we seem to think that God will create a "force field" that will protect you from physical or psychological harm. This is not true and no one should expect that because it has serious implications, especially after tragedy. Indeed, it will cause a crisis of faith.

---

[95] Rodney Kleyn. "Why Do the Righteous Suffer? (Job#1)." Last modified February, 2, 2014, http://www.prca.org/resources/sermons/reading/item/3527-why-do-the-righteous-suffer-job-1

We are unable to see as God sees, and we should trust that He is working everything for our good. Often this is through suffering and tragedy, as well as, through love and joy. Almost every biblical theophany began with "be not afraid."[96] Be not afraid was not a guarantee that you will never be subjected to pain and suffering. Be not afraid is calling you to trust in God no matter what else happens, He is with you; He is taking care of you; He loves you and He is working His plan for His glory and ours.

The Protoevangelium (Protoevangelium, the first Gospel. The first promise of Redemption. Gen. 3:15) displays God's mercy and how He uses everything for good, especially evil. God did not defeat the suffering that was ushered in with sin. Instead, He did something greater; He used sin to bring man/woman in greater communion with God, into the very life of God.

We know through divine revelation that suffering and death entered the human condition with original sin. God made creation and when He saw what He had done "it was good."[97] Disobedience caused the fall, but God created a greater destiny for man/woman after the fall. God made man's destiny even better because God is always working for good.

In *O Felix Culpa!* Father Ray Ryland explains how God blessed us through the fall.

> "O happy fault, O necessary sin of Adam which gained for us so great a Redeemer!"
>
> God created man in His own image and loved him with infinite love. God gave man free will, with the capacity to respond freely to God. Man misused that free will to rebel against God, and thereby infected the human race with original sin.
>
> Why, then, does the Church through her liturgy dare to speak of the fall as a "happy fault" or a "necessary sin?"
>
> Had our first parents not fallen by sin, they would have remained in a state of supernatural grace. Eventually they would have been taken into heaven, and would have shared in the vision of God. For

---

96 Gen. 45:5 Douay Version.
97 Gen. 1:10 New Revised Standard Version Bible: Catholic Edition.

unfallen persons, that would be the deepest possible union between God and human beings.

Now again, why does the Church lead us to rejoice in the fall of the human race? The reason is that through the redemption of Jesus Christ we have been restored to the supernatural state in a way far surpassing in glory what we could have known had there been no fall.[98]

God uses everything for good. The theophany, "be not afraid"[99] must be interpreted in light of this reality. God does not say that everything will be joyful and devoid of suffering. In fact, you may suffer greatly, but you should still "be not afraid"[100] because no matter what happens whether it's horrific or wonderful, God will make it a blessing. He can be trusted in all things, good and bad.

---

98 Ray Ryland. "O Felix Culpa! Oh Happy Fault!" Accessed November 13, 2016 http://chnetwork.org/2012/04/03/o-felix-culpa-oh-happy-fault-by-fr-ray-ryland/
99 Gen. 45:5 Douay Version.
100 Gen 45:5

Be Not Afraid

Pray, hope, and don't worry.

—Padre Pio[101]

Christ was fully aware that all men/women will experience suffering (albeit in different degrees). It seems counterintuitive to say not to be afraid with the knowledge that all will suffer. With this knowledge, we must deduce that His words do not mean that suffering will not occur. Indeed it will. Christ proclaims "be not afraid"[102] to the Apostles and most of them would be martyred through horrific suffering. "Peace I leave with you; my peace I give to you."[103] Peace means something different. The peace of Christ is a peace that realizes that Christ will use everything for good; therefore, peace is a state of trust. Peace is felt more deeply by those who have faced immense hardship and suffering. Meet every situation with great peace; no matter what happens in life, good or bad, say amen, so be it. God will make it good and trusting in Him gives you great peace!

---

101 Joseph Pronechen. "Pray, Hope, and Dont Worry." Accessed February, 14, 2017. http://www.catholiceducation.org/en/faith-and-character/faith-and-character/pray-hope-and-dont-worry.html
102 Luke 12:4 Douay Version.
103 John 14:27 New Revised Standard Version Bible: Catholic Edition.

I remember the day after the accident; Father Crawford told me that the accident and death of Angel is part of Divine Providence. I remember those were the only words of comfort that I had received. In fact, those words brought me peace and refuge. God was in control and I can trust Him. This peace was so very important in my first days of grief. In time, it is obvious that I started to question God's goodness, but God was calling me to a deeper understanding that was only possible *through doubt*. A deeper understanding brings a deeper peace; it's all a gift. <u>Through my struggle, I have grown closer to God, much closer.</u> Now, I love and trust Him whereas before I just feared Him.

I once read that faith is the absence of anxiety. The modern idea of faith equates certitude to faith and this is not the true definition of faith. Faith must be accompanied with an element of doubt because otherwise it's mere knowledge (perhaps incorrect knowledge, but not faith). I had the wrong idea of faith. I too thought that faith meant that one is positive about a belief. Faith is so much greater than being certain. In fact, faith is a theological virtue (Theological virtues: The theological virtues, faith, hope and love relate directly to God as their origin, motive and object) and certitude is not. "Now faith is confidence in what we hope for and assurance about what we do not see."[104] True faith is the peace that Christ gave us; it is His gift to us.

---

104 Heb. 11:1.

The Fallacy of Control

Control is an illusion.

—Ward Ketring

I REMEMBER THE night of the accident looking over at Ward and realizing that there was nothing Ward could do. There was nothing that anyone could do to save her. Ward realized with such clarity that we do not have control and all security is an illusion. So, if we are not in control, who is? Is God in control? Where does God's will end and free will begin? Does God will evil to derive good? I believe the answer is no. I do think that God intervenes in our lives and He cooperates with our bad and destructive choices, as well as our good choices. I do believe He is God and He is able to derive good from even the worst situation. I believe we can choose whether or not to allow the good to manifest in our lives, but even if we do not cooperate with good, God can still create opportunities of good even after a long line of bad choices. Dom Hubert van Seller wrote, "Even for the collapses that we are manifestly to blame—even our sins—can be turned into good account. There is nothing so bad that it cannot be taken up by grace and made into a potential good."[105] God does not will evil, but He will use it and defeat it and make it good.

---

[105] Dom Hubert Van Zeller, *Suffering: The Catholic Answer* (Manchester, NH: Sophia Institute Press, 2002), 24.

AN ANGEL OF THE BEATITUDES

Did God will the death of my sweet Angel? I do believe that it is part of Divine Providence, but that does not mean that I particularly believe that her death at that moment was His will. I believe that her death is working toward good, the more we cooperate with the good, the more good will come. God's Providence is larger than any particular situation and when we attempt to look at the particular (Angel's death) we are too limited. Surely our actions have natural consequences; we are not mere puppets. It seems that God uses everything and molds it toward good. This is the action of an omnipotent loving God. Salvation history is connected by many particular situations, but the story never ends with a particular situation. In other words, we are unable to see the full context of the particular because it is a part of a cohesive whole that is still unfolding. Furthermore, our limited understanding is skewed by sin, and we are unable to see reality as it truly is and we attempt to put God in this context, instead of realizing that it is a limitation of our perspective. This is the problem of attempting to discern if something that feels terrible is God's will or a victim of chance. Terrible things do happen and I believe God weeps with us. I believe that God and His plan are more powerful than any horrific tragedy. Many terrible things are a direct consequence of an action or sin that often becomes destructive. This does not mean that God is not in control because He is always ultimately in control; however, He grants our free will that disorders the good that God gives us, and He chooses to work with our bad (and good) choices to unfold salvation history. It seems that in the big picture of God's Divine Providence He will use everything for good, even evil. Only God can do that!

So do I believe that it's God's will or not? As Saint Augustine taught, God does not allow anything to happen that He cannot derive a greater good. I believe that our lives are in God's hands and He works with our free will. I believe that God's Wisdom chose for Angel to go into eternity in cooperation with the free will of all involved because He is molding this tragedy into His Providence for the greatest good. Yes, God is in control, but He cooperates with us, always working for good according to His purpose. Only God is able to take any choice that we make and turn it into good. He makes all things new. I also realized that heaven in never a punishment! In fact, taking Angel into divine love is a blessing. There is nothing we can do that God cannot turn it into His glory. God is always trustworthy. This reality makes this world a different place and it alleviates so much anxiety because you are able to trust in any situation.

Saint Francis was walking with a friend and got to a fork in the road. Francis said to his friend, "Spin me around and whatever road I face will be the road God wants me to go down."[106] Saint Francis knew that God is down both roads. Of course some paths are better for you than others, but there is a deep peace in realizing that God will be wherever you are. St. Paul says, "That all things work for good for those who love God, who are called according to his purpose."[107]

Beautiful!

---

[106] Rom. 8:28.
[107] Ibid.

Where is Heaven?

> Christ's Ascension means that he no longer belongs to
> the world of corruption and death that conditions our
> life. It means that he belongs entirely to God. He, the
> Eternal Son, led our human existence into God's presence,
> taking with him flesh and blood in a transfigured form.
>
> —Pope Benedict XVI[108]

Haunting questions have entered my mind. I've been somewhat preoccupied with "where is heaven?" and "what is heaven?" Both are important questions, especially if your child is "there." I have a great fear that my hope is a comfort and nothing more. Why won't God just show us the truth, so we may know? If it was real, God would not be hidden. If it were truth, it would not be disguised. If the dead were alive, why won't they communicate with the living? Despair begins to conquer my mind with two problems. Why isn't the spiritual reality around us visible? If there is indeed life after death, where is heaven?

In antiquity, it was believed that one must get closer to God and this is why the patriarchs and profits would always climb a mountain to be "closer

---

108 Pope Benedict XVI, *The Joy of Knowing Christ* (Frederick, Maryland: The Word Among Us Press, 2009), 138.

to God." Metaphorically, I see the value of expressing all creatures are in fact beneath God. I think the motion has value as an act of humility, but I do not think that one is literally closer to God when they are in a higher latitude. It seems that we still take this somewhat literally and we see heaven as a place "up there." The implications of this form of thinking literally separate heaven and earth.

It seems that life and death have been consigned to places (i.e. earth is for the living while heaven is for the dead) and this understanding mythicizes its reality. How is heaven to be described by limited human language? It is impossible to describe what I do not know, but revelation leads me to an understanding of the condition of life after death that I can comprehend.

Heaven and earth are not two separate places as if there are boundaries that border one from the other. Perhaps we do not "go to heaven" but rather, we are no longer conditioned by sin and death, so we can actually see what is veiled in our condition. It seems that our senses are skewed when sin conditions us. There are things we do not hear, see, taste, feel or smell that are all around us. Some animals have senses that work differently or some have an entirely new sense. Perhaps our senses are either conditioned by sin or not yet fully realized or both. Maybe the distortion of senses is a form of division that will be reconciled. Possibly, when we walk into eternity, we walk into a state of being that is no longer divided, like flesh and spirit. We are body/souls as a unity that is a whole person. Your heavenly body is a visible sign of your truest self. Nothing is hidden, but truth is what guides this state or condition.

The Body of Christ is not limited to time or space and I am part of the Body of Christ. I, along with the ecclesiastical community, am part of His body. When I help anyone in need, I help Angel because she is one with Him. I have unlimited access to her through my beloved Lord Jesus Christ. Heaven is here right now. Theologically, I knew that I had access to Angel through the Eucharist. In fact, I even said to Father Tim at her death bedside that I can still be close to her through the Eucharist. I thank God that I knew that as truth because it was an instantaneous comfort, but I did not even come close to truly comprehending it. Baby is with God, but she is with me too. Heaven is reconciliation, not division. Angel is not "divided" from me because that contradicts union. Angel is truly present, not as a memory or as a thought, but as a person. I have access to her through Him. He is "with us always"[109] and Angel is no longer divided from God. She is part of Him just as I am part of Him; in Him we are one. This is not figurative language, but a reality. Of course God is not limited to Angel any more than God is limited to me. Through Him, with Him, and in unity with Him I have access to her, and I presently continue my relationship with my sweet Angel.

Often people believe that "healing after death" requires a "letting go." I contend that it is not a "letting go," but that it is a realization that there is life beyond our senses. The very life of God that surrounds us. Jesus did not leave us. He did not come to prove something and leave so we may know about Him and simply gain access to heaven.

The Pharisees witnessed many signs and miracles, yet many refused to believe. Obviously, seeing does not equate to believing. Belief, in the transcendent is not a mere result of verified facts. One may remain blind after "seeing" and one may see without witnessing. Faith must be an intrinsic part of knowledge for your eyes to be opened beyond the limits of human knowledge. In this life, seeing is subjective. Heaven is being part of the very life of God, part of the exchange of love. We refer to heaven as a place, "up there." Sometimes "when we get there" is referenced and this implies a place. A specific place is constrained to time and space. Due to our finite minds, we make heaven into an eternal "place." Perhaps we think of it as a celestial place, but this seems to limit the totality of heaven and it separates heaven and earth. Perhaps, when a person is in heaven, he or she is in an uninhibited state of being, a condition that is not distorted by sin and death. Perhaps, the immortal person is in a real state of being that far exceeds our senses. Perhaps, my sweet Angel is right here with me in a very real way. Sometimes people say that she lives in my heart and that is far too abstract, too unreal. She is alive and her life goes far beyond my heart.

"Being asked by the Pharisees when the Kingdom of God would come," he answered them, "The Kingdom of God doesn't come with observation;

---

109 Matt. 28:20.

neither will they say, 'Look, here!' or, 'Look, there!' for behold, the Kingdom of God is within you."[110]

My love of God and my love of Angel are now intertwined because Angel is with God. When I could tangibly hold and kiss my Sweet Little Love, my love for her was not completely intermingled with my love of God. Although all my love has God as its source, and love is never excluded for love, my love of Angel is intertwined with my love of God because He is my access to her. She is not divided from Him because of her heavenly union with Him. Love of God and love of Angel are now intertwined.

Inside our very being is love, and we desire love as our deepest longing. Our deepest desire is invisible. Love is invisible, yet it is very real. Perhaps the most precious things are invisible. This realization is important to me because I am unable to see my beloved and I sometimes fear that invisible equates to nonexistent. When I contemplate love, I realize that the highest order of things is not visible. "For ever since the world was created, people have seen the earth and sky. Through everything God made, they can clearly see his invisible qualities—his eternal power and divine nature. So they have no excuse for not knowing God."[111]

Love, the invisible, is our highest calling. Our love is not limited to our senses or limited to this life. I fell in love with Angel before she ever took her first breath, before I could see her. I loved her every day of her earthly life, and I continue to love her after she has taken her last breath. My love for her continues to grow and flourish. I am far too small to encompass all my love; my love is greater than me. My earthly body is unable to encompass my love because it is limited to my finite being. My love is beyond my visible body. Angel is part of divine love; therefore, it is impossible for me to "see" her. I can see the "invisible qualities" of God in created things and know that she is with Him.

My priest, Father Bernie, was saying a funeral mass for a parishioner who had aged and slowly declined in health. I remember he said that the aging process and the decline of health allow more room for God. As we age, we

---

110 Luke 17:20–21.
111 Rom. 1:20.

physically "empty" ourselves and make more room for God. I was so touched by the positive perspective on the decline of health that our culture views as shameful. This made me realize that God emptied Himself to become man, His kenosis.[112] God was invisible, but when He emptied Himself He became visible, incarnate. Perhaps, our "process of divinization" our pleroo (Pleroo-Greek-to make full/to fill to the full)[113] makes us beyond human sight, like God before His kenosis. The infinite cannot be seen. A book titled *Heaven Sense* explains the invisible infinite. "The infinite has no parts. The infinite cannot be divided. One cannot see half of it, or a third, or a tenth; one either sees it as a unity in its entirety, or one does not see it at all. The infinite exceeds the finite not in extent, but in innermost being."[114] Perhaps it is invisible because it is impossible, in our finiteness, to see the infinite.

---

112 Kenosis," Theopedia, accessed June 29, 2017, http://www.theopedia.com/kenosis

113 "Pleroo," Bible Study Tools, accessed June 29, 2017, http://www.biblestudytools.com/lexicons/greek/nas/pleroo.html

114 John Peter Arendzen, *Heaven Sense*, (Manchester, NH: Sophia Institute Press, 2004), 9.

A Child of the Beatitudes

I want to spend my heaven doing good on earth.

—Saint Therese of Lisieux[115]

It is so human to want or even expect answers. We want to know why this had to happen. Yet healing does not come from the explained; it comes from trusting in God when He seems untrustworthy. For me, I had to realize that Angel's future in heaven is a *future worth living. It is not a wasted future.* Of course it is not the future I dreamed of for her. I had to acquiesce to the will of the Father. When your child enters eternity there is an extreme amount of disappointment. This is a constant battle that I continue to fight.

I am still on my earthly pilgrimage and my faith story will continue, maybe eternally. Through my reflections I have come to believe that my pain is edifying to me and the Body of Christ. My pain has a beautiful purpose and it is not wasted. I am in my dark night and all I can do is surrender it to the Lord. The deepest faith emerges from the darkest night. I've learned that God's love is complex and it doesn't always feel like love. Christ told us that the way is hard, but we do not want to hear that we must face difficulty, we

---

[115] John Clarke, trans., *The Story of a Soul: The Autobiography of St Thérèse of Lisieux* (Washington D.C.: ICS Publications, 1975), PAGE NUMBER.

AN ANGEL OF THE BEATITUDES

must carry our cross. God is the source of all that is good and suffering feels that it separates us from happiness. We are unable to see the blessing of suffering in the middle of our dark night. When we allow God to transform our suffering, it becomes our greatest glory. Christ, when allowed, transforms all suffering and the cross becomes a triumphant symbol. Suddenly, the absurdity of worshiping a victim on a cross becomes comprehensible. The Cross becomes hopeful.

Angel, the child I literally risked my own life to have, continues to hold my entire capacity of love. I've always told all my children that I love each of them with all my heart. I hate the thought of excluding her from my earthly life, so I don't. I have her belongings and I treasure them because they are hers. They are tangible. My Catholic faith taught me this—to use images, relics, and ceremony to express the inexpressible. To use the visible to express the invisible. There is a great line of demarcation in my life before the accident and after. I am forever changed and I trust that God is working that for His Glory. He makes all things new and I must trust in His plan. It is a feat to trust God when He seems so untrustworthy. My greatest and deepest fear was realized on that night, and I relied on God. It's hard to trust, but I still do. I am not in control and all I can do is surrender to God. For the first time in my life, I just gave it all to God because it was too much for me. *I surrender to Him and trust that He will use everything for good.* I trust my love still has the person Angel as its object. I keep Angel close to me through prayer, remembering, and the Eucharist. I do not believe in death; I believe in eternal life! My hope is that everything is leading us to union and love has the last word. Angel is alive, living a meaningful life of service and Love. This journey, my journey, will be complete when full union is achieved and life comes from life and into eternal happiness.

Jesus taught us the Beatitudes in His great Sermon on the Mount. Jesus taught me the Beatitudes and Angel showed me how to live them.

Blessed are the poor in spirit, for theirs is the kingdom of heaven.
Blessed are they who mourn, for they shall be comforted.
Blessed are the meek, for they shall inherit the earth.

Blessed are they who hunger and thirst for righteousness, for they shall be satisfied.
Blessed are the merciful, for they shall obtain mercy.
Blessed are the pure of heart, for they shall see God.
Blessed are the peacemakers, for they shall be called children of God.
Blessed are they who are persecuted for the sake of righteousness, for theirs is the kingdom of heaven.[116]

God's ways are so far beyond human comprehension and it seems that God works in impossible ways. This is why the Beatitudes are so difficult, they seem counterintuitive and it seems that many see it as a fulfillment that will occur in the next life instead of being instructive for happiness in this life. The Catechism explains the Beatitudes: "The Beatitudes fulfill the promises by ordering them no longer merely to the possession of a territory, but to the kingdom of heaven. They express the vocation of the faithful associated with the glory of His Passion and Resurrection; they shed light on the actions and attitudes characteristic of the Christian life; they are the paradoxical promises that sustain hope in the midst of tribulations; they proclaim the blessings and rewards already secured, however dimly, for Christ's disciples; they have begun in the lives of the Virgin Mary and all the saints."[117] We, all Christians, are people of the Beatitudes. The Beatitudes are instructive for all life, our earthly and our heavenly lives. "God put us in the world to know, to love, and to serve Him, and so to come to paradise. Beatitude makes us "partakers of the divine nature" and of eternal life.[118] With beatitude, man enters into the glory of Christ and into the joy of the Trinitarian life." [119] The Beatitudes show us how God makes all things new and He can be trusted in all things, especially

---

116 Matt. 5:3–10.
117 IntraText Editorial Staff, eds., *Catechism of the Catholic Church*. (Citta del Vaticano: Libreria Editrice Vaticana, 1993), accessed November 11, 2016, http://www.vatican.va/archive/ENG0015/_INDEX.HTM#fonte.
118 Ibid.
119 Ibid.

the most difficult tribulations. Angel's short earthly life was imperfectly lived with great fidelity to the Beatitudes because she lived the Greatest Commandment, the Commandment of Love, with faithfulness and grace.

> **Blessed are the poor in spirit, for theirs is the kingdom of heaven.**
> As a child of the Beatitudes, you lived God's Kingdom with love and joy.
> **Blessed are the meek, for they shall inherit the earth.**
> You did not seek to be higher than anyone; you understood that no one was higher than you. You were not greedy, you just enjoyed life.
> **Blessed are they who mourn, for they shall be comforted.**
> You lamented other people's pain.
> **Blessed are they who hunger and thirst for righteousness, for they shall be satisfied.**
> You wanted a just world and participated in ensuing justice.
> **Blessed are the merciful, for they shall obtain mercy.**
> Your mercy was severe.
> **Blessed are the pure of heart, for they shall see God.**
> You were modest and pure.
> **Blessed are the peacemakers, for they shall be called children of God.**
> You always sought peace and understood its value.
> **Blessed are they who are persecuted for the sake of righteousness, for theirs is the kingdom of heaven.**
> You would give yourself for another, even if it was not deserved. Indeed, you would suffer persecution for injustice as well as justice.

In spite of all the pain that I feel for my great loss, I know that I am equally blessed with great joy. I know that God is transforming all of my pain into love and it benefits the entire Communion of Saints, including myself and Angel. God blessed our lives by giving us Angel, even though we had to endure her death. Angel is the happiest child I have ever encountered. When she was little, I even called her my Joy Baby. She always reflects beatitude/

happiness because blessedness is just part of her. In the final analysis, Angel is a gift and she remains a gift; she is a Child of the Beatitudes. She remains a gift; not because she blessed my life for fifteen years, **but because she blesses me for all eternity; my eternal gift.**

Ward, Emily, Carmina, Angel, and John
The Ketring Family

Matthew 23:27 Jesus denouncing Pharisees as "whitewashed tombs" and "hypocrites."